SO-AHJ-677

# Meditation:
# The Journey to Your Inner World

## *Eidan Or*

Meditation is the way to new consciousness. It is the way to achieve awareness, to live serenely, to make the most of your powers of concentration, and to develop your character.

This book discusses the spiritual and philosophical basis of meditation, with an emphasis on the underlying principles. Above all, it provides instruction, including tried and true exercises, for using meditation in the best and most effective way for our benefit.

The importance of this book lies in the bridge it creates between the spiritual ideas and practical everyday use appropriate for everyone. Even readers unfamiliar with the spiritual theories underlying meditations will be able to use the book effectively and benefit from it.

**Eidan Or** came to the world of mediation at a relatively late age, after completing his army service and studying philosophy at university. His curiosity took him as far as India, where he spent three years studying meditation and yoga before becoming a qualified teacher. He has taught yoga and meditation and various centers in France, Germany and the USA, before settling in Israel in a remote village in the Galilee (a stone's throw from where Jesus spent his youth). Here he has established a spiritual center where he teaches his students meditation on a high level and serves as their spiritual teacher.

Livonia Public Library
ALFRED NOBLE BRANCH
32901 PLYMOUTH ROAD
Livonia, Michigan 48150-1793
421-6600
LIVN #19

158.12
0

## ASTROLOG COMPLETE GUIDES SERIES

The Complete Guide to Coffee Grounds and Tea Leaf Reading
*Sara Zed*

The Complete Guide to Palmistry
*Batia Shorek*

The Complete Guide to Tarot Reading
*Hali Morag*

Crystals — Types, Use and Meaning
*Connie Islin*

The Dictionary of Dreams
*Eili Goldberg*

Meditation: The Journey to Your Inner World
*Eidan Or*

# MEDITATION

## The Journey To Your Inner Self

### Idan Or

Livonia Public Library
ALFRED NOBLE BRANCH
32901 PLYMOUTH ROAD
Livonia, Michigan 48150-1793
421-6600
LIVN #19

Astrolog Publishing House

Astrolog Publishing House

P.O.Box 1123, Hod Hasharon 45111, Israel

TEL/FAX. 972-9-7412044

E-Mail: info@astrolog.co.il

Astrolog Web Site: www.astrolog.co.il

꒰MAY 1 7 2000

©Idan Or 1998

ISBN 965-494-008-6

All rights reserved. No part of this publication may be reproduced,
stored in a retrieval system, or transmitted, in any form or by any
means, electronic, mechanical, photocopying, recording or otherwise,
without the prior permission of the publisher.

Published by Astrolog Publishing House 1998

Distribution:
U.S.A & CANADA by APG - associated publishers group
U.K & EUROPE by DEEP BOOKS
EAST ASIA by CKK Ltd

Printed in Israel

10 9 8 7 6 5 4 3 2 1

3 9082 07819 5339

# Chapters

In order to make the most of this book, we recommend that readers first browse through the entire book in order to become familiar with its contents. You may then go on to read the various chapters (not necessarily in order).

After reading each chapter, we recommend that you take a little time to reflect on what you have read before moving on to the next chapter.

At a later stage, as you begin practical exercises, it is worth reading the appropriate chapters again in order to discover the inner truth in keeping with your own inner world.

## The Inner Ability in each of us

How often have you said to yourself, "If only I could, I would do this or that?" And how many times have you been left with no more than the aspiration, without making any serious effort to realize your goal? The inner power to realize and achieve your aspirations, wishes, and desires depends on you and you alone. The inner belief in your ability to translate your yearning for something into concrete reality can be found only inside yourself.

In order to be able to make the first step toward realizing your objectives, you must first of all believe in yourself and your ability to act. Why do you always believe that others can "do it," and that it is only you who will never succeed?

The first reason is that you do not have enough faith in yourself. The reasons for this could lie in all the factors responsible for the development of your personality: family, environment, experiences, and, of course, your own character. For some of us, all these factors have led us to develop an inferior and poor self-image. We lack basic security in ourselves and our abilities. If you do not do it, no one else can restore your self-image. Even if you use the services of professionals trained to delve into the past and retrieve pieces of information to help you attempt to redevelop your personality, the inner work itself will always be left to you.

The most important thing is to think positively, and to try to adopt an optimistic approach to life. If you do this, it will be relatively easy to overcome obstacles, instead of allowing a dark veil to descend and obscure the reality in which you find yourself.

You should always think about the strong anchors that provide you with powerful and secure support. Whenever you feel as though you are being swept away into despair of frustration, think about these anchors. Almost all of us have some kind of support on which we can rely. This is your own private anchor.

The anchor is something that you can always think of in times of distress as a positive, strong force reinforcing you and restoring your inner calm. Your anchor might be a supportive family: the irreplaceable strength that comes from warm and loving parents, a loving spouse, or adorable children; it might be a stable and positive work environment; or a special home to which you love to return.

The more you believe in yourself and your ability, the more able you will be to achieve the things you desire. The next most important factor is the determination to move toward the objective you have chosen, and to persist in your path. If you can use determination to remove the obstacles in your path, you will already have taken the main step toward achieving your objective. Overcoming obstacles requires considerable effort and mental strength. These can only be achieved if you believe in your own inner ability.

Even after overcoming the difficulties preventing you from achieving your goal, you must continue to think positively and not to be drawn off into side roads or into injuring others on the way to achieving your objective. If you manage to do this, you will surely be successful and reach your desired goal.

In order to be capable of controlling your nerves and achieving calm and relaxation, you must learn self-control and self-discipline. This will be possible only if you exercise these faculties at each stage and during every action you perform in your everyday life.

As your self-awareness grows, your ability to look inside yourself will also develop.

This will enable you to achieve complete control over every step you take, since these steps will be made calmly and with inner peace, secure in the knowledge that your decisions are correct.

This enables you to realize that your ability is unlimited; as the saying goes, "the sky is the limit!"

When you become aware that you are wise, strong, and have a dominant personality with its own force to shape its world, it will be easier for you to accept the fact that if you can do this, so can everyone else around you.

The world is full of people at least as beautiful, wise, and strong as you — sometimes more so. Recognizing your own ability and those of others will also enable you to look at the world in a more relaxed manner, encouraging you to respect other people and their needs, desires, and abilities.

One of the most important elements in developing yourself, understanding the needs of others, and creating a positive world is the ability to love, to do good, and, of course, to accept love in return.

As you move toward achieving your goal, it is important to remember to use anything that can be helpful to you and draw you closer to your objective. Any means is acceptable in so doing, provided that you use honest and brave steps, and not actions requiring you to trample on others or exploit them.

The way to achieve your goals must be free of any taint of evil or machination. As long as you are honest with yourself and with those around you, every step you take to draw yourself closer to your goal will also contribute to others and, in the final analysis, will be a blessing to them as well.

## Persistence in reaching your goal

Whatever your objective may be, you must be determined to achieve it at almost any price. Persistent belief in your own ability is the only way to achieve your objective. Determination and the ability to concentrate your whole being on your goal will eventually enable you to reach your objective.

As you move toward achieving your goal, you will encounter all kinds of distractions and disturbances that may sometimes frustrate you or cause anxiety. Each time this happens you must recoup your inner strengths to help you overcome the obstacles. If you allow yourself to be distracted, you will become extremely frustrated.

You must draw not only on your mental capacities but also on your physical strength, devoting all your actions to one direction. This will eventually enable you to be what you really want to be, or to achieve what you really want in life.

If you are hot-tempered or easily angered, you must practice your ability to remain cool even in situations where you feel emotionally suffocated and long to express what you really feel. The ability to remain alert and to control all your senses and actions may be extremely useful, particularly in long-term planning.

People who have reached a high status in life and managed to attain positions of power or influence, to become famous, and to serve as a model for others have usually done so not only because of their capabilities, but more importantly because of their hard work and almost uncompromising determination.

The more you demand of yourself and refuse to give in, and the more you manage not to wallow in self-pity in times of crisis or spoil yourself too much, the nearer you will come to achieving the goals you set yourself, until you eventually reach your target.

## Controlling what happens to us

We cannot control everything that happens to us, but in many areas of life we can guide and help determine events around us.

Studies have proven the connection between body and soul. People whose souls are dominated by chaos and who cannot find anything to hang on to; people who are confused and cannot concentrate on themselves and work out what they really want; people who are not reconciled with themselves and whose mental calm has been disturbed for any reason and are subject to stress; or people dominated by a feeling of guilt or anxiety — are all liable to be more vulnerable to disease and natural injury than those who enjoy mental resilience.

Our character is in part determined and modeled according to our ability to control our inner selves, our intellect, and our entire being. Without a conscious clarification of the desires that guide us in life, we will be rootless and inclined to lose touch with ourselves. In order to be capable of meeting our tasks we must forge the path for ourselves and determine what our motives are for achieving the goals we have set.

The ability to act calmly in progressing toward our objectives can be achieved through practice. Practice is achieved by training our brain and associated faculties such as memory, perception, concentration, and so on.

## Freeing ourselves of egotistical needs

In order to enhance our powers of concentration we must be practice coping with everyday situations. As we direct our whole being to thinking optimistically and positively, we must release the stress around us and attempt to achieve as calm a state of mind as possible.

Looking at situations from an positive starting point and being willing to accept reality from a forgiving world view will develop an ability in us to accept others with love, instead of concentrating only on our own personal situation. This will enable us to be more attentive to the needs of the world around us. As we learn to accept others with open arms, we will gradually free ourselves of our own egotistical needs and learn to ignore our private pleasures and the satisfaction of our personal desires and wishes. As we open up to the world and to others around us, and learn to concentrate less on our own personal needs, we will be free to concentrate on pure and noble thoughts.

Concentration and subsequently meditation enable us to embark on an inner journey, drawing nearer to the consciousness and the entity inherent within us all. This process will not only enable us to experience the inner processes within us, but will also assuage accumulated stress, and calm and help us relax our muscles and even reduce our anxiety level, regulating blood pressure, drawing our attention away from bodily pains such as headaches, and helping us achieve both mental and physical release.

Concentrating on a single point, whether physically or through inner reflection, eliminating transient thoughts that pass through our mind, and directing ourselves to our inner core all require extensive practice.

The more we persist in this, the more we will be able to reach a state in which our thoughts will no longer wander or disturb our concentration. We will not be distracted by everything that happens around us, and thus will be free to soar beyond our consciousness. According to the principles of Indian yoga, at the final and highest stage of reflection and concentration we will achieve a state where the soul leaves the body and flies to planes of supreme wisdom beyond ourselves.

The supreme capacity of concentration, usually achieved only after practice, enables busy people and those who work in demanding positions requiring long and exhausting hours to live fuller lives. Taking time out to practice supreme concentration demands that we close off all our senses to the environment and concentrate on a single point, thus enhancing our wisdom, calm, control, and the fountain of love and acceptance.

Those who experience this exercise on a daily basis report that it heightens their senses and thinking, creating a sense of freshness, optimism, and an ability to continue their daily lives with enhanced energy and alertness.

## Process of thinking and concentration

The thoughts that pass through our minds are part of an associative process. We can change the course of these thoughts and determine which we wish to develop and which to ignore, which to address in depth and which to put on the side for later consideration. As we think we unconsciously take steps to direct our concentration as we wish from one thought to another.

We cannot control what type of thought comes into our mind or what associations it arouses, but we can certainly intervene in the rhythm of our thoughts, developing particular areas or completely ignoring others.

When practicing concentration we must allow our thoughts to run freely around our minds, while we stand on the side as observers, following them as if they were a separate entity and not part of our being.

Then the process of selection begins. From the jumble of thoughts passing before our eyes, we choose that thought on which we wish to concentrate. We must then concentrate on the associations this thought evokes.

If, for example, our intervention in our though process has led us to focus on a thought about walking to the sea, we must then set in motion the associations, visual pictures, and thoughts evoked in us by the word "sea." Naturally we shall immediately see images such as sand, boats, bathing suits, ice-cream, and so on, and will feel certain emotions we feel about the sea, such as joy or dislike. After "running" these associations through our mind, we must once again intervene in our thought process in order to select an association or thought out of those that emerged in us, and then repeat the process again and again.

In this type of process we ourselves set the rhythm of our thoughts. Through this artificial intervention in the process of bringing up associations and pictures, we effectively channel the process and thus gain control of the entire process.

The recognition that this process may also take the place of our own free will and that it may be controlled will be a previously unknown experience for us and will enhance our self-control. Self-control provides not only confidence, but also a sense of strength and of being able to manage events rather than take them for granted.

## Practicing concentration

After understanding and discussing the thought processes we can now move on to practicing concentration. How can we prevent our thoughts from wandering during the process of concentration? How can we overcome distractions and focus our thoughts on a single, consecutive continuum?

A number of methods exist for practicing concentration. After completing this process and learning the ability to focus on a specific subject without being distracted or diverted, we will be able to combine our entire being, body and soul, into a harmonious and united whole. This will eventually lead us to calm and peace.

Practicing concentration cannot be achieved in a short period of time but requires concentrated practice over a period of days and even months.

Choose a particular object, concentrate on it, and try to think of every association it evokes. Stretch your mind in order to think of the remotest possible associations that occur to you. For example, let us take the word "sea." What associations occur to you when you imagine the sea or think about it? Try to run through your mind's eye everything that you automatically and instinctively associate with the word "sea." You will probably think of such associations as beach, boat, sand, rocks, sunset, and so on — items that belong to the panorama of your imagination. You will also no doubt think of words such as sunshade, ice-cream, bathing suit, beach balls, and so on — objects that are associated with going to the sea. You will also probably think of words relating to sensations associated with the sea: warmth, calm, love, romance, peace, desire, and so on.

If you are not a sea-lover and the associations you think of when you imagine the sea are unpleasant or uncomfortable, choose another word you feel comfortable with and have a positive attitude toward. The goal is to use the concentration exercise to achieve harmony, pleasantness, peace, and calm — not the reverse.

The exercise of thinking of associations connected with the word "sea" is not over when you believe you have completed the list. You must try to repeat the exercise again and again over a number of days or weeks. Every time you think of the word "sea," repeat the associations you have already thought of and try to bring up new ones to add to your list. You might like to write down all the associations you have thought of, and then add new ones, even if your list contains as many as a hundred words, until you cannot think of any more associative words.

Remember to return every so often to the word "sea," rather than allowing yourself to be tempted off on a mystery trail from the other words contemplated. Make sure to keep the word you started with at the center, rather than being dragged off on other paths.

Each time you repeat this exercise, you must reproduce memory processes. Over time as you repeat the exercise you will be able to follow the workings of your brain as it brings these pieces of memory back to your consciousness, and thus practice the sense of power you feel every time this process occurs in your brain.

In addition to practicing memory and concentration, another process occurs as you observe the "drawers" in which your brain stores its data bases.

Remember that during the exercise you must be relaxed and let the flow sweep you along. You must not resist or adopt a negative or alienated perspective, since this will prevent your achieving the desired objective. In order to learn techniques for penetrating through our consciousness and the inner processes that occur in our brains, we must open ourselves up to understanding these processes and accept them lovingly and happily.

If after a few weeks or a month you manage to bring yourself to a state of concentration on a given topic after an average period of a few minutes (between 5 and 20 on average), you will have achieved a real breakthrough in acquiring the habits of meditation.

## Atmosphere and position during concentration exercises and meditation

In practicing concentration exercises, we must first choose an appropriate location.

It is important to choose a calm and quiet place where we know we will not be disturbed during the exercise by telephone calls or people entering the room. It is equally important that you feel that the room has a pleasant and enjoyable atmosphere. You should feel that you would like to spend the amount of time in the room required for the exercise or meditation.

In order to feel as comfortable as possible when you are practicing meditation, it is also important to be dressed comfortably. It is a good idea to wear comfortable and slightly baggy clothes. If you have the chance to change out of your work clothes into meditation clothes, that is ideal. If you cannot do so, at least loosen your belt, open a button or two, or unfasten your tie. The goal is to feel as comfortable as possible; our bodies should be relaxed and unpressured.

Before moving on to select the position in which we will sit, it is worth deciding what object we are going to concentrate on, and what the subject of our concentration will be. Having chosen our subject, we can be sure that we will not be distracted or diverted during the concentration, because we will already be sure of our subject. Remember to choose an object you love or one that makes you feel good and pleasant that you really want to connect to during the time you have set aside.

The period of time involved may range from a few minutes to a longer period of up to thirty minutes or so. You should also set the interval in advance, adding a little more time each time you practice. This is due both to the difficulty you will find in keeping your attention on one subject during the first times you practice concentration, and also the difficulty everyone encounters in holding their body in a particular physical position of sitting for a long period of concentration.

The position you are going to sit in is also something that should be chosen before you begin, and you should decide that this will be your permanent meditation position from now on. It is not a good idea to choose to lie down, since this encourages one to become unfocused, to lose alertness, and to feel sleepy.

A seated position is the best, preferably without the support of cushions or a chair back. Those who find this very difficult or who suffer from severe back pain may support the lower back with cushions in order to make it easier to sit up for a long period.

You should sit up straight and tall but not tensely. Your head should form a straight line with your neck but should be relaxed. Do not strain your muscles. Place your hands in any position that allows them to be relaxed and lets the blood flow freely without pressure or tension.

The more you practice your chosen meditation position, and the more persistent you are, the easier you will find it to maintain the position for extended periods, even if you feel some pain to begin with. Do not attach too much attention to this — over time, as your muscles get used to your chosen position, the pain will disappear.

## Pay attention to your breathing

In order to achieve a high level of concentration and focus on your insight and inner consciousness, it is a good idea to listen to the rhythm of your breathing. As you practice inner concentration, let your breathing take place of its own accord. Do not participate actively in the breathing process, but let your body shape the process by itself, leading you instead of you leading it. This will allow you to breathe in a relaxed manner instead of through inner tension.

Follow the air as it enters your stomach. Feel how it fills you. Let your breaths be long and deep. Then follow the air as it leaves your body. Notice the warmth of the air as it leaves your body and the moist expiration that accompanies it.

Do not try artificially to force air into your 'stomach'. Just let your breathing be regular and calm, as it is usually, yet within the process of meditation be aware of your breath and concentrate on it.

# Frequency of practicing concentration and meditation

There are no laws in meditation. You can practice it once a day or more often, or just once or twice a week. It all depends on how willing you are and how great is your need and desire for meditation. In order to achieve real results, it is usually worth persisting with daily exercises that will eventually become a part of your routine. Exercising just once or twice a week will make it harder for you to get used to the process and to achieve a high level of concentration within a limited period of time.

The secret to achieving good results, as in anything in life, is to practice as intensively as possible, every day.

The number of times you choose to meditate and enter deep concentration is up to you.

Most people choose to take time out in this way once a day, though some feel the need to practice concentration twice a day. Few people would require more than this. Those who practice meditation twice a day are usually those who have been practicing it for years and can easily enter a state of deep concentration and remain in this state for a short period of time each time.

There are no laws as to how many times you choose to meditate. You should listen to yourself and adjust your meditation to your personal needs.

The same applies to the time of the exercise. Some people need just a few minutes in order to refresh themselves and accumulate renewed force, calm down, and become relaxed. Others need a longer period of concentration and take longer to move through all the stages of meditation up to achieving maximum concentration.

The function of meditation is to lead us to harmony with ourselves and the world around us, to penetrate the inner layers of our consciousness and to renew our inner energies.

Since we practice meditation solely in order to recharge our positive forces, we must listen to our bodies and our needs. Each of us must decide how long to devote to meditation according to what they feel is right for themselves.

It is usually a good idea to stick to a set period of time and to try not to go beyond this limit. In the future this will help to make meditation part of a daily routine as we get used to daily exercises.

Meditation should eventually become an integral part of daily life. If we manage to keep a set time frame for exercises we will find it easier to make meditation part of our life.

If we go beyond our set limit every day, this may lead us to lose control of other activities that we no longer have time for due to our meditation. This may in turn lead to pressure or tension because of our failure to divide our time properly.

It would be a mistake to start meditating without setting a time limit, unless you feel that your physical and mental state on a particular day mean that you need to allocate some special additional time for meditation — if this is the case, you should take it into account in advance.

# What is the best time of day to meditate?

This, too, is a matter of individual preference. Each of us will find a different time when they feel comfortable and can enter a state of meditation and concentration.

Some people find the morning the best time, and prefer to meditate early when they are fresh, before beginning the packed daily routine awaiting them. This enables them to start the day calm, full of energy and dynamism.

Others find that in the morning they have to rush to get everything done before they go to work, and have no time to devote to meditation within their packed schedule. Even if such people were willing and able to make time to meditate in the morning, they would be disturbed by all the thoughts they have to deal with before beginning their working day — thoughts that would swirl around their mind and prevent them from concentrating. Thus they could never achieve any level of concentration in meditation.

Some people who are particularly busy, usually those in senior positions, advocate the practice of meditation at midday, providing a break within their busy daily routine and tight schedule. Such people usually find a short period of time during their day in the office, close the door, and ask the secretary not to forward telephone calls for the next 15 minutes. They should then loosen their clothes a little, take off their jacket, unfasten their tie, open a button in their shirt, and practice meditation in full comfort.

This approach, of meditating at midday during work, can help prevent the stress that builds up during the day. Creating an artificial interruption in the work day to close out the voices around us, concentrate on our inner self, and achieve a sense of peace and calm, can often be more valuable than a good sleep in recharging our batteries and helping us get through the work day, not only full of renewed positive energy but also more relaxed and calm. Executives and those in senior positions who have to supervise work teams can then return to work refreshed and act more pleasantly toward the employees around them. Not only they will benefit from this, but also will the workers with whom they come into contact. Reducing the tensions that accumulate at work during the morning is very important to continuing the day successfully.

People who are able to organize the time to meditate every day at work should try hard to persist. It is important to persevere, and it is worth setting a fixed time every day rather than moving the meditation time around from day to day. When we get used to meditating at a given time each day, our body and soul adjust to this by a kind of internal biological clock, and it becomes another normal part of the things we are used to doing every day. If we miss out one day, we will feel it strongly and miss the experience, just as if we are used to brushing our teeth twice a day and forget to do so we feel uncomfortable or tense in some way, or just as those who are used to beginning the day with a cup of coffee feel slightly nervous if they miss it one morning.

Some people choose the evening as the best time to meditate. They feel that only then can they really get into a state of concentration, free of all the daily activities that might disturb them and impair their concentration at other times.

It is very important to make sure that you do not

choose too late a time in the evening, since it is all too easy to be swept from meditation into a deep sleep. This will blur the thoughts and make it very difficult to think clearly and concentrate on the object you have chosen.

If it is easier for you to concentrate in the evening, choose a time when you are still fully alert.

For example, it would not be a good idea to choose to meditate after eating dinner and when you have not eaten a real meal all day. At such a time your inner energies are focusing on digesting food, and you enter a kind of state of post-mealtime lethargy. This lethargy makes it all too easy to fall asleep, and that much more difficult to remain alert and focused.

We may lose sight of the purpose of our meditation if we leave the exercise until late in the evening. Apart from inner observation and focusing on our selves, part of the power of the meditation experience is to bring body and soul to a new level of positive energetic capacity.

If we do not leave ourselves the chance after meditating to enjoy several hours of pleasant and tension-free evening time, a large part of the force of this experience will be lost.

## Consistency in exercise

We often find that what is really difficult is not so much learning to meditate and achieving a high level of concentration and inner observation, but rather to persist in practicing meditation over the course of time.

Some people start off full of excitement about their new abilities and describe the wonders of meditation in enchanting terms, but this level of enthusiasm quickly wears off.

Why does this happen? What is it that makes people stop doing something even though they love it, and what is the secret of consistency and persistence?

Strength of character certainly exerts a strong influence on the ability to persist, but other factors also lead people who very much enjoyed practicing meditation to stop exercising.

In order to be consistent we should pay attention to the factors we discussed above, particularly the time we choose to practice meditation. Selecting the wrong time, or one that is inappropriate for us, will quickly lead to increasing gaps between sessions until they drop off completely.

If you feel that meditation has become a chore at the time you chose, change the time. Try another more appropriate time, and if that is also inconvenient try again, and so on until you find the best time of day for you to meditate.

Similarly, the problem might be that the place where you have chosen to practice meditation does not provide the calm you need in order to enter a state of concentration. Here, too, try to find other more suitable places or positions. Try to make the time you devote to meditation more pleasant by lighting sweet-smelling incense or dimming the lights in the room where you practice so that the pleasant atmosphere will help you to feel comfortable.

Without perseverance you cannot experience the real meaning of meditation and reach the higher states of concentration of consciousness.

## Can I really do it?

Some people doubt their ability to concentrate, even if they have a genuine inner desire to experience this state.

Just as you can concentrate on the various tasks you perform during the day, whether they are voluntary or otherwise, so you must realize that you have the basic ability inside you to do this, as does every individual. Were it not for our capacity to concentrate we could not manage our world. We need a measure of concentration in order to plan how to carry out our everyday tasks. We concentrate even when we perform the simplest of routine tasks such as deciding what cycle to use in the washing machine, not to mention complex decisions requiring prolonged concentration on a completely different level, such as when reading a book or watching a film.

During meditation we direct our inherent capacity to concentrate inside, into our soul and consciousness, into our inner being and core.

In most cases, this is far from a simple task. We are not used to looking inside ourselves or accustomed to this type of concentration, which demands a process that is the opposite of what we have been used to all our lives. Now we must develop a capacity of concentration that flows from ourselves inwards, rather than outwards.

During the early stages of meditation, you may encounter difficulties that will make you feel like giving up. You must remember that in order to achieve positive results, we must go one step at a time. There's no need to rush. If you expect instant results you are bound to be disappointed.

As with any process, positive results or successes are achieved after intensive training and work.

Do not tell yourself "I'll never make it" as soon as you begin to practice.

Do not say "I wasn't made for this," or "I can't get what I want from it."

When we make such comments, we are denying our potential to open up to the process before we have really gotten started.

Meditation is a world in itself, and it cannot be encompassed and embraced in a single moment. Move into this world with all the curiosity in you, take a deep breath, and begin to explore it slowly. Each time another layer will be revealed, and you will slowly contact this world and feel more and more that you are part of it, and that it is part of you.

## How do we carry out thinking exercises?

The process of thinking actually consists of a series of ideas that develop and move on rapidly from one to the next. We are "carried" by our consciousness from one thought or idea to the next, like a body endlessly drifting on the ocean.

The associative process is also a type of thought process, but while it stems from our subconscious and is beyond our control, our ideas and thoughts are voluntary.

We can direct our thought, "fast forward," or "rewind" slowly. We can replay sections of thought or make ourselves embark on a "journey" through new thoughts and original ideas.

The origin of thought processes and the flow of ideas lies in associations that rise from the subconscious to the consciousness.

As with any physical process, we are completely aware of the action we are undertaking, but we are unaware of the entire cerebral process that takes place in our minds that has caused us to perform this action.

In order to be capable of taking in the world, we cannot concentrate on everything at once, since we do not have the capacity to contain the entire world. What we can do is to concentrate on specific sections, on aspects that are accessible and comprehensible to us, and use our thoughts to move from one idea to the next.

Through our consciousness we realize that in objective terms there are an infinite number of ideas that exist in a complete and spacious world.

Yet through our mind, which enables us to reach certain levels of our consciousness, we can only become acquainted with part of the thoughts or ideas that accompany us through this spacious world.

Ideas cannot follow one another except through associative connections. Each thought leads to the next according to a consecutive rationale. There can be no transitions without order and no gaps in the sequences.

The connections lead step by step from one idea to the next, without skipping.

There are an infinite number of possible conceptual or associative connections of this kind that may lead in all kind of directions, such as:

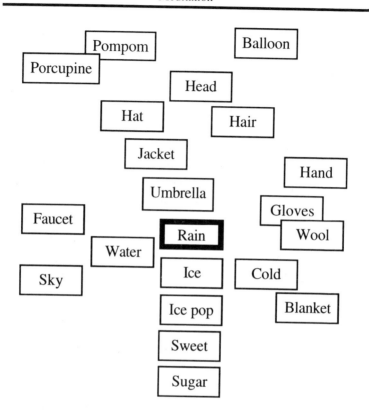

You can direct your thoughts in whatever direction you want, but allowing yourself to "cruise" the depths of your consciousness will expand your horizons and enable you to become better acquainted with your innermost self.

The more you explore your infinite world of thought, the broader your horizons will be, as far as their limits.

## Trends of thought

Naturally the journey our thought takes in our consciousness, and the conscious and unconscious selection of how to move from one idea to the next, will be partly dependent on our own character, tendencies, and the areas of emotional importance to us. Different people think of different associations. Each person has their own private world and their own world of associations.

When someone who is involved in the world of dance thinks about the word "muscle," they will think about movement. A butcher will think immediately about the different parts of the cow that he sells.

We can try to take control of our associations and steer them in a particular direction, according to our state of consciousness. This may be achieved by directing our thoughts when we are in a state of deep concentration.

For example, if we decided to focus on the word "brotherhood," the associative process might raise such words as "peace," "college," and "soldiers." We might then use the thought process to think about these words in terms of the word "brotherhood." For example, "peace" might make us think about brotherhood between all people. "College" makes us think of one of the fraternities some students join to seek camaraderie and friendship. And how can we get from "soldiers" to "brotherhood?" The stages might be: "soldiers" — "war" — "danger" — "partnership in danger" — "brotherhood."

Naturally one could find many other examples of this process. Each person has their own affinity with the subject of the concentration exercise and their own private world of associations.

## Concentrating on the purpose in order to achieve the goal

Meditation itself, in the course of which we use techniques of concentration, can teach us to direct and focus ourselves on achieving a particular desire and purpose we wish to reach in life.

Whatever the goal we wish to reach, the purpose of our life is that which we seek to develop. Our goals may change, and as we realize old goals new ones will immediately emerge. Yet the purpose toward which we work is that to which we must always direct ourselves.

Most of us probably have a few basic goals we hope to achieve in life. Indeed, we can probably assume that most of us have rather similar goals, such as to be loved, to establish a family, to be capable of providing for ourselves and our family, to live in a pleasant and attractive home, and to be content with the work we do. On the narrower level, however, we all have our own specific aspirations and desires that reflect our own distinct personalities.

Some people direct their lives in such a manner as to enable them to reach a senior position in their work as they possess good managerial skills; others spend their entire lives striving to acquire as much property or money as possible, as this lends them a sense of security; and others seek to realize the goal of being able to travel around the world as much as they desire.

In order to realize our current goals, or others that emerge as we go through life, we must create an initial state of consciousness characterized by a specific internal atmosphere toward which we direct ourselves and upon which we concentrate.

Meditation helps us to create a static state of consciousness and awareness that will accompany us as we move toward success, and help keep us targeted on the task we have decided to accomplish.

We should not look at everything we do in life solely in terms of our goal; if we do so, we may find that we miss much of the good that comes along with achieving the purpose of our life. If we always see no more than our goal before us, we will not notice the small things of daily life that serve as the foundation stones in the purpose toward which we are working,

The difference between focusing solely on the goal and looking beyond to our purpose is analogous to the difference between always looking outward and looking inward to our inner self.

In order to achieve our purpose, and not only our goal, we must be open to the idea of giving. If we give of ourselves to others, if we are sensitive of others' problems, and if we examine the abundant inner good that lies within each one of us, we will have achieved three-fourths of the struggle for success.

If we believe strongly enough in ourselves and our own ability, it is reasonable to assume that we will be able to cope with anything that comes our way as we move toward success.

It is not advisable to delude ourselves that by being

egocentric and measuring success solely in terms of material goods and the external trappings of honor, status or money, we will be able to succeed.

The opposite is the case. If the only thing that can offer you security are these external trappings, your underlying security will vanish the day you lose your job, or whatever it is that enables you to achieve these trappings of success. Real success is measured by the extent of your inner strength and the security that stems from your own autonomy.

Once your security is dependent on external trappings, the loss of these trappings will cause alarm, pressure, anxiety, and severe emotional distress.

If your basic security does not depend on any external factor but on your inner personality, nothing can shake it or make you lose your inherent emotional powers.

You must rid yourself of those feelings that make you imagine that you are superior to those who surround you. If the only way you can feel superiority and pride is by oppressing other people, you are missing the true meaning of life.

The superiority and pride you feel are no more than an illusion. Each of us must allow each other person their own space and freedom, and to let others feel their own strength. That is the only way you, too, will feel your own strength. Feelings such as hatred, jealousy, anxiety, and malice are the result of extreme pride. To rid ourselves of such feelings, we must distance them from our consciousness. Only in this way will you maintain your own autonomy, positive thinking, and capacity to give.

Achieving control over our desires and mental actions

can only be achieved if our state of consciousness is stable and uninterrupted.

Persisting in such a mental state will gradually enable us to open up to others, leading us to act kindly and purely toward them, and thus strengthening both our own ego and those around us.

## Using resources wisely and efficiently

The more we disperse our forces, rather than concentrating them toward our own benefit, the more we lose important energies that we could have exploited in our own favor in order to achieve our purpose.

In order to prevent such a "waste" of energies, we should direct our actions to achieve benefit and avoid idleness. It is important to distinguish between idleness and rest; the latter is certainly positive per se and should not be avoided. There is also a positive type of idleness — one that has an inherent purpose.

Our daily schedule is important and we should always plan what we are doing. There is no need to go overboard and start planning what we will do every single hour of the day, but we should certainly get up in the morning with the feeling that we have a structured and organized day ahead of us, and that we know what the division of time is between the different activities that comprise our day. This will, for example, prevent us from lounging around in bed until a late hour of the morning, which is one of the worst ways to waste our time and energy.

Time is a precious resource, and it is worth learning to

use it to the full. For example, pieces of "dead" time over which we have no control, such as waiting in line for the bus or the doctor, can be used to the full if we read a book or study some more material for an upcoming examination.

We must be efficient, however, not only in using our time to the best effect, but also in many other areas: eating properly, at the right time, and in the quantity needed by our bodies; knowing how to listen to others and to really hear what they are saying; knowing how to choose what field we should work in and how not to waste our resources on areas that are inappropriate for us; knowing when we are stubbornly trying to achieve something that we do not need, leading to the pointless loss of energy; and knowing when we are entering a difficult emotional state dominated by feelings of tension, fear, or nerves. Such a state can lead to considerable physical discomfort, and such negative thoughts should therefore be eliminated.

It is also worth freeing ourselves of urges that are not associated with any clearly-defined purpose, since these reduce our determination and internal willpower. The pleasures and desires inside us should be consonant with our purposes and goals.

## Regular mental exercise

The use of special concentration exercises is completely unlike the normal thought process we use in everyday situations. Training and exercising the brain cannot be achieved by reading books, making calculations, trying to sharpen our memory, and so on. Mental practice that takes place in a controlled and directed manner for a short period of time every day leads to an increase in our ability to control our brain that goes far beyond what any other everyday action can provide.

There is no comparison between regular, directed, and focused exercise and the many simple tasks the brain performs in the normal domain, since in the latter we are more concerned with our worries and with finding solutions than with practice and direction.

In order to exercise our mind, we must firstly enable ourselves to achieve bodily calm. In order to begin to exercise our brain without interruption and achieve the maximum possible results from the exercise, our body must be calm, relaxed, and peaceful in physical terms.

Mental exercise should take place only after the pre-condition of maximum bodily rest has been achieved.

When the body is relaxed, this automatically leads to a reduction in mental strains or excitement. Muscle strain is also reduced.

When the body is quiet, our minds can be active, thus enabling the exercise to achieve the best possible effect.

Constant exercise of the mind in order to maximize concentration thus requires an ability to restrain our physical impulses, to repress superfluous excitement that distracts us from the main task at hand, to limit our aspirations, desires, or surprise at shocking incidents.

This might seem an impossible task, but if we are faithful to the principle of efficiency and of confining our actions to achieve our purpose, we will always keep our ideal goal in front of us as we move forward.

Persisting in exercise will also enable us to see the beauty that is to be found along the way to success, not only the beauty that comes from reaching success itself.

## Preparing for concentration exercises

We already discussed the need to be in a comfortable and optimal position when engaging in meditation exercises in the chapter "Atmosphere and position during concentration exercises and meditation."

Before beginning the exercises, it is very important to get our body used to spending several minutes in a static state, without disturbance or change. Take a period of about two weeks to a month (depending on your physical state) and begin to practice the sitting position you have chosen for meditation. In this way, when you begin the meditation exercises as such you will not feel uncomfortable at having to sit in that position for a long time, and you will not be disturbed by sensations of discomfort that might disrupt the concentration you achieve through the exercises.

If you do not want to practice the sitting position at the very beginning, you might begin instead with other exercises in which the body is still, such as standing still for several minutes (three to five) in a state of complete rest, without moving at all. Let your muscles relax and be sure to free the tension in your neck and shoulders. Every so often think again about your neck and shoulders and release them again if necessary. Often the tension returns very quickly to these parts of the body, particularly among those who are not trained in relaxation. While standing like this, do not ask yourself whether or not it is a pleasant position. Cast your thoughts far beyond the position in which you are standing. Do not pay attention to little twinges or itches, to pain or tickling sensations, and try not to raise your hand to scratch yourself. Stay still without moving. The only part of your body that should move is your chest, rising and falling with each breath according to the rhythm of the esophagus.

It is also worthwhile to practice complete relaxation of the body:

Lie on the floor, preferably on a carpet or a hard mattress, in a pleasant and comfortable spot. Do not lie on a thick mattress that will allow you to sink down. Choose a relatively hard place on which to recline, and begin to relax every part of your body.

Begin with your toes: feel how they relax. Continue to your feet. Once again, try to relax the muscles and let your feet fall to the side in a state of complete relaxation. Continue up your shins, knees, thighs, buttocks, and stomach. Gradually release each of these parts of your body.

Let your arms fall to either side of your body. Now relax your fingertips and knuckles, your wrists, arms, and shoulders. Continue up, relaxing your chest and breathing out. Breathe deeply and slowly. Now move on to your head. Relax your neck muscles, lips, cheeks, eyelids (closed), nose, forehead, and skull. Lastly imagine that your body is sinking slowly into the ground, and that the ground is wrapping around you. Try to dwell on your relaxed body and listen to your slow breathing.

In order to enter a state of concentration, we must also practice breathing, which will be of great importance in the advanced stages of entering deep states of concentration. It is important to breathe deeply and slowly. While practicing breathing, pay attention to the position of your chest. It should be open to receive as much air as possible directed into your lungs. This is why it is so important to keep your back straight. A bent back restricts the capacity of the lungs. Breathe through your nose, and make sure to keep your mouth closed during the exercises.

Once you are sitting in a relaxed position and have opened your chest, begin to practice breathing. First empty your lungs in one breath, then take a full breath but slowly, not all at once. When you feel that your lungs are filled to capacity, slowly exhale the air. Do not fill your lungs too much, and do not retain the air in your lungs for too long. Practice breathing just as you do normally, but more slowly and thoroughly. We must breathe naturally — otherwise we will be more preoccupied with our breathing than with the object on which we wish to concentrate, which would miss the main point.

Unlike the other preparatory exercises, you do not have to fix a set hour for breathing exercises. You do not have to do them at home — other possibilities are on the bus, while walking, sitting, reading, or watching television.

You can also use special tension and relaxation exercises for particular muscle groups, for example for the neck muscles or for the face and eye muscles.

### Exercise for the neck muscles:

To exercise your neck muscles, sit comfortably and stretch your neck as far as you can. Then relax slowly.

Stretch again, and now roll your head down, to the left, around, and to the right in a circular motion. As you move your neck back, make sure to keep your neck muscles slightly tense so that your neck does not fall back too suddenly. These exercises should be performed slowly. Be aware of each stage. Then you can move your neck to the left and back to the center, to the right and back to the center again.

### Eye exercises:
Eye exercises should be performed slowly and calmly.

Sit comfortably with some object in front of you. Move your eyes over the contours of the object. Firstly start with both eyes on one side of the object, and then on the other. Now close your eyes and let them relax. Open your eyes and let your gaze climb up to the ceiling and then down to the floor. Now draw your gaze to the left and to the far left end of the room and then to the right and the far right end of the room.

In addition to the preparatory exercises for meditation, we also recommend strongly that you engage in some form of sport in order to maintain the body in a correct, flexible, and stable state. Short daily exercises lasting a few minutes, or exercise lasting about one hour twice a week, will eventually lead you to much better results in meditation — and indeed in life in general.

# Developing an ability to ignore interruptions

We cannot always find a quiet corner at home that is completely free of interruptions. Even if you close yourself in a room in privacy, there will still be external noises that you cannot control and that may make it hard for you to concentrate, such as members of your family walking around the house and talking; a cat or dog; a phone ringing; noises from the outside, such as cars or children playing, and so on.

It may sound difficult or even impossible to completely ignore these noises, but we have conclusive proof that this can be done. Every one of us has at sometime experienced the state of daydreaming, reading a fascinating book, or listening to a radio program when we became oblivious to external interruptions. While daydreaming, for example, we can hear the noises around us and see what is going on, but we are not conscious of these things, because our mind is "elsewhere." If someone asks us later who walked past us or what happened while we were daydreaming, we will not be able to tell them.

How can we train ourselves to ignore noises and voices as we do when daydreaming?

Firstly, we have to be sure that we do not anticipate any disturbance while carrying out our concentration exercise. Do not attempt to begin a concentration exercise if you know that a guest will soon be arriving or a member of your family is about to come home. If you know in advance that such an interruption is expected, you will be unable even to begin to concentrate. Your senses will be too alert to every outside noise.

Having made sure that no interruption is expected, begin your exercise: Choose a noise you can hear, such as the ticking of a clock or the dripping of a faucet. While concentrating, try to ignore the presence of that sound. Try not to hear it. Gradually listen only to your body and yourself, and imagine other sounds. Slowly immerse the ticking of the clock or the dripping of the faucet into the sounds you have created in your imagination until the noise disappears and becomes completely blurred.

If you persist in these exercises, you will eventually attain a state of complete concentration, and you will be able to continue uninterrupted even if your concentration exercise is disturbed.

## How can you avoid bothersome thoughts?

Thoughts that preoccupy your mind and disturb you when you are trying to concentrate on meditation do not come of their own accord. If you can usually manage to ignore your thoughts and concentrate, but occasionally find that you cannot escape your wandering thoughts, there is probably a reason why.

It is very hard to sit and practice meditation if you are constantly being bothered by an irritating thought. If you are aware that there is some problem that has been bothering you all day, such as something that happened at work or at home, financial worries, or so on, it is well worth trying to sit down and work through the problem so that you can reach some type of solution, such as "I have to do x, and tomorrow I will get around to it," or "I should be able to solve the problem with a telephone call" (in which case you should make the call before you go on to practice concentration, so that you can begin fresh and clear).

If despite this you begin a concentration exercise and find that particular thoughts refuse to leave you, although you try to ignore them, tell yourself that as soon as you finish the exercise you will deal with these thoughts (and do so).

By postponing the task, rather than ignoring it, you ensure that the matter has been temporarily resolved, and will now find it easier to return to your concentration.

If despite all your best efforts to ignore external noises or interruptions you are unable to do so, try to change the place where you exercise. You may not always be aware of the influence a particular place has on your functional abilities. Try to think of personal experiences you have had during your life in which a particular place exerted a welcome or oppressive influence.

For example, when you were at school or college there was probably one room at home where you found it easiest to concentrate on your studies than elsewhere. Perhaps you preferred to study in the garden rather than inside. Sometimes the pleasant atmosphere of a room may be due to the presence of objects you like or particular items of furniture you find pleasant, despite the fact that the room is rather noisy, whereas another, quieter room does not give you the inner atmosphere you need in order to concentrate.

You must choose wherever you find it easiest to concentrate. Above all, the point is that you must find it pleasant to spend time in the room and it must make you feel relaxed and calm.

If possible, try to arrange a quiet room that you can use as a special place for concentration. You can place objects in the room that you like, or objects on which you may wish to concentrate during your exercises. Arrange the room as your own little corner of paradise, with attractive rugs, cushions, and curtains to make your stay in the room special and pleasant. If you like, use your favorite incense in the room, or place candles of different shapes and colors around the room to light during concentration, in order to help you achieve an atmosphere of inner focus.

If you can do so, it is worth setting time aside to bathe before beginning your concentration exercise. This will make you feel cleaner and purer physically, something that often promotes a purer mental feeling due to the strong connection between body and mind. You may choose to wear special clothes for meditation; these should be light and airy, and preferably made from cotton. Natural fibers are preferable to synthetic ones, offering a more pleasant and comfortable feeling.

The mere fact of engaging in all these special preparations also helps to prepare your inner awareness gradually for the concentration time. This will help you ignore external noises and interruptions and focus more quickly and easily on your exercise.

## Practicing consistent thought

How do our minds think?
How do ideas emerge in our thoughts?
If we examine our thought process and break it down

into sections in order to understand its workings, we will find that in order for a thought process to occur, at least two ideas must be combined in our mind. It is the connection and progress of these ideas that creates the process. Thinking not only enables us to play around with ideas. On completing the thought process, we can reach conclusions, learn new things, make new discoveries, and thus invent new things or reach new insights.

In order to achieve conceptual stability and to unify our ideas, we need to concentrate. Our ability to concentrate will be greater the more our thought process is strong, stable, and free of digression.

When practicing thought processes (as we shall see below in the exercises), we train ourselves to simplify and shorten the thought process, so that it is consecutive and free of distractions. Those not trained in thought processes may reach the same solution to a given problem as those who do have such experience, but undoubtedly the latter will so more easily and rapidly.

How can we practice thought processes?

The fact is that we can use these exercises in any state or situation. We do not need a special place or atmosphere in order to exercise this faculty.

Essentially these exercises enable us to be much more consistent in our thought processes, and more aware of the process itself.

The following exercises illustrate how we can move through our thoughts while concentrating. It is important to achieve at least a measure of concentration before beginning these exercises.

**Try to practice the following exercises:**

* Think about the journey you make every day from home to work. If you use the bus, try to recreate the path you take from your home to the bus stop, getting on the bus, choosing a seat, the people around you as you travel, the sights you pass. Imagine the noise of the motor stopping at the bus stops and continuing on its way. Then imagine the point where you get off the bus, walk to your place of work, go into the building, go up or down the steps or in the elevator, and the places you pass until you arrive at your work place, put on your overalls, or sit down to begin work.

Now try to recreate the way back home at the end of your day's work.

* You could use the same technique to recreate your daily walk with your dog. Concentrate on the tiniest of details along the way you know so well. Then recreate the way back home.

**Now try some exercises in visual perception:**

* Try to imagine a row of objects, for example: a ring, a window, a television screen, a dog (or any other animal), and so on. Now try to examine what size the objects were when you thought of them. Where they the same size as in reality, or did you magnify or reduce their real size? Now try to deliberately reduce the size of these objects, and then to magnify them.

Now think of the same objects again, or of different objects. Try to gradually remove different parts of them in your mind until they disappear completely from your imaginary screen.

For example, say that you chose to imagine an airplane. Imagine it with a different part removed each time. First remove one wing, then the other. Now remove the tail, the cockpit, and lastly the body of the plane. After practicing this, try the process in reverse. First imagine the body of the plane, then one wing, then the second wing, and so on.

* A similar exercise, but one requiring broader spatial perception: Imagine a picture with which you are very familiar. Now try to remove different details in the picture as in the previous example. For example, firstly remove the background, then the different items in the picture, until you can see no more than the frame. Then reverse the exercise: Begin to fill the picture with its different component parts. Bring back one detail after another until the picture is once again complete.

* Choose a specific object to concentrate on, such as a wall clock. Now try to imagine yourself examining the clock from every possible angle. First look at it face on, then from the side, but seeing more than just its outline. Now try to imagine how it looks from above. Imagine that you can rise above the clock and look down on it. Now "enter" the wall on which the clock hangs and look at it from behind. Imagine any buttons or wheels it has on its reverse side. Then "dive" down and look at it from the bottom up. After this exercise, try to imagine the clock simultaneously from all these angles until you build a precise three-dimensional image in your mind.

* You have already experienced magnifying and reducing objects. In this exercise, choose particular objects and leave them at their real size, but in your imagination

reduce yourself to the size needed to enable you to enter the objects.

For example, think about one of the drawers in your clothes closet. Now imagine yourself small enough to be able to enter the drawer and walk around. Imagine the feel of your clothes. Walk from one side to the other; check whether there are little particles of dust, an opening, or a handle. How does the drawer look from the inside? What can you see out of the crack looking from the inside out?

After completing the exercise, gradually restore yourself to your true size. Now try the opposite process: magnify yourself to enormous proportions. When you are about as big as the closet itself, look down at the drawer, which will now look much smaller than its true proportions.

Repeat these exercises several times using different objects.

The type of exercises describe above will help us to concentrate our thoughts and control our thought processes. Instead of wandering aimlessly from thought to thought, we will have a clear, sharp, and consistent direction. When our thoughts appear in a logical and directed sequence instead of in a random jumble, we will find it easier to concentrate on objects and ideas, to imagine mental pictures, and to ignore external noises and interruptions that might otherwise disturb our concentration.

## The transition to meditation

Mediation as the direct continuation of concentration exercises is a kind of journey — a journey into our inner consciousness, and an insight into the being and life that fills us.

Meditation is also a type of experience in which we intensify our mutual relationships with the world.

When we stand in awe at the beauty of the world, at its sparkle or the vitality with which it inspires us, we internalize this profound experience that makes us want to encompass the world with love and joy. This experience will always accompany us. We will always be able to relive it inside, since it has become part of us. We will not lose this experience and it will not diminish in strength as long as it is powerfully engraved in our memory.

When we imagine and relive this powerful and beautiful experience, we experience once again the mood that accompanied it. Almost automatically we find ourselves at peace with the world, and the feelings of love and beauty that we felt the first time resurface once again. We experience a supreme sense of devotion and a desire to blend with nature and our environment. This teaches us in a direct manner such characteristics as modesty, humility, and so forth, removing arrogance, pride, and the desire to rebel against the world. This is the essence of meditation.

# How can we know that we are practicing meditation?

Meditation, the next stage after the concentration exercises, means the ability to achieve inner concentration at the highest possible level; the ability to look inside our consciousness and our inner being.

This does not imply some kind of drowsiness or blurring of the senses; far from it. Indeed, meditation is a state of supreme alertness, with a strong dimension of inner intent. The optimal state of meditation is one of inner focus and maintenance of a constant intention within our own awareness.

During meditation we are not in a state of what others may see as a "trance," such as the mental state of hypnosis whereby willpower is detached from the body. Neither are we in a state of deep sleep or disconnected from the world in any way. On the contrary, we are well aware of where we are, focused inside at the highest possible level of concentration we can achieve at each stage until we reach the maximum possible level of insight.

Meditation brings us to a kind of supreme consciousness. This is the highest stage of awareness we can experience: the zenith of our consciousness, the perfection of concentration that brings new forces to our existential being.

## The power of meditation

A person who does not practice meditation may be likened to a shallow stream. Water tends to lose direction and to spill out of the course of the stream, mixing with the water from other streams. The flow is influenced by the wind, by the vegetation around it, and by other factors that divert it from its clear course.

By contrast, a person who engages consistently in meditation is analogous to a deep stream, flowing in a single, clear, distinct course. If he diverts from his course, he immediately sets himself back on course. Sure in his direction, he is not so easily influenced by external factors.

The high level of concentration achieved through meditation leads to a higher level of awareness. In this way we can be more sure of ourselves, instead of being swept away by the latest fashion or craze in all kinds of confusing directions. We can be calm in the knowledge that we are in control.

Meditation is the ability to develop our creative capacity without disturbance, to eliminate anxiety and fear, to achieve peace and calm, to release pressure, to experience sensations of uplifting and happiness, to reduce our blood pressure by natural means, and to develop our physical and mental capacities. Eventually, this process can lead us to enlightenment and to spiritual heights that each individual can interpret as they wish.

## Freedom from thought

After repeated practice of meditation, usually after numerous times that we have worked to achieve constantly higher levels of concentration, we will feel that our concentration is so strong that at some stage we stop following our transient thoughts and they stop emerging in our mind.

Our awareness will be devoted entirely to the experience, to the point that we will be unable even to halt during the experience and think "Wow! I am not bothered by my thought any more" — since that is in itself a transient thought. We will only be able to experience this state as it is, without interpreting it.

This stage is total immersion of the consciousness within the limits of our existing ego, distinct from our thoughts.

You cannot describe this experience until you have actually experienced it, but it possesses a kind of perfection and unity that enables us to realize that there is no separation between ourselves and our awareness. This is a unique moment and it is usually felt by experienced people who have been practicing meditation for a long time. Anyone can achieve this state; it is not dependent on any special emotional, intellectual, or other capacities.

Our conscious awareness during meditation is at a high level of alertness, focus, and concentration, and yet it is in a calm and carefree state. The immediate connection between conscious awareness and our sub-conscious, over which we have no control, sometimes leads to a state where after meditation we find that we can solve problems that were previously beyond our coping powers.

The clarity of awareness achieved during meditation is like the sharp clarity of a lake or the sea. The waves and the rising sand cloud the water. Only after the swirling of the water has stopped and the water is still again, only after the sand has sunk to the bottom again and the water is clear, can we see the depths. Sometimes the water is so clean and still that we almost imagine it has disappeared, since now it is hardly visible.

The thoughts and preoccupations that move around our mind are like the grains of sand rising to the surface of the water, preventing us from clearly seeing the bottom of the sea.

As we get used to meditation, we leave our thoughts behind and focus. Slowly everything inside us sinks, and we can see it all clearly and sharply. Everything is laid out before us purely and cleanly, without disturbance or dirt.

After exercising, it is always a good idea to examine what kind of thoughts occurred to us while meditating. Did we generally have positive thoughts that made us approach the world around us and the people with whom we come into contact in a positive manner? Did we have thoughts that relate to the way we look at the world based on a positive values system, or were most of our thoughts negative?

Were our thoughts accompanied by pleasant feelings, or were our feelings dominated by sorrow, pangs of conscience, regret, or jealousy toward the world around us?

Such introspection will enable us to gain insight into our real nature. Thus we will be able to appreciate the thoughts and moods that accompany us every day, almost without our ever having noticed.

In meditation, and particularly as we reach an advanced stage, we may sometimes experience periods when we manage to reach a level of concentration that prevents any thoughts. Yet occasionally thoughts may arise without our being able to control or ignore them. If they come on the flow of our thoughts, pass by and do not disturb us, we should let them float on and wait for the next wave of thoughts. However, if these thoughts bother us and make us physically uncomfortable, it is worth examining their origin and working hard inside ourselves to solve the problem or issue that we face.

## Achieving insight

Even after inner observation has led us to a state of calm, our brain will still be bothered by passing thoughts. We must let these thoughts come and go without trying to fight them. Along with calm will come insight.

What is insight? It is the ability to examine thoroughly the nature of any object, animate or inanimate, and to adopt its reality as if it were something familiar and well known to us. When we practice meditation, what we are effectively doing is examining our own being and nature. We embark on a journey inside ourselves, into our consciousness and the depths of our being. As we examine ourselves, we also examine the world in which we live and the different facets of its autonomy and personality, as if from a distance. We can see ourselves from perspectives that cannot be experienced when we are hampered by everyday activities. Our insight can be focused on different parts of our body, and we can become aware of the processes occurring within us.

Our body is the physical home of our spirit and soul and of all that accompanies them in our consciousness, awareness, insight, and being. Since the body complements these other elements, when we are attentive to it and learn to accept it lovingly and joyfully, we can enable ourselves to feel a sense of harmony and unity of body and spirit.

Our ability to enjoy what our body has to offer us and to experience it peacefully and amicably is extremely important. People who practice meditation regularly generally feel more comfortable with their body.

As our insight develops, so does our sense of awareness of our own existence. There are various levels of insight, and when we manage to reach the higher levels we attain a high level of awareness of the calm and peaceful core within us, and are able to focus on this core without distraction.

During the process of insight, we do not shirk from close examination and investigation of aspects relating to our emotions and feelings. We can examine these areas and discover that negative feelings or pains are the result of the way we categorize our emotions. As we re-examine these feelings in a balanced and open way, we come to see that fear, anxiety, tension, or jealousy are all emotions that through level-headed examination can come to be seen as less threatening than we had imagined. Thus we can come to accept these emotions, too, with love, and to dissipate the associated tension.

# Coping with feelings

During meditation we will sometimes find ourselves dominated by various feelings. In some cases we will be able to overcome and ignore these feelings, which will then dissipate and blend back into us. In other cases, however, particular feelings may overcome us without our being able to ignore them or postpone them for later consideration. We feel the full force of these feelings in an experiential manner. We can feel the sensation rising in us and filling our entire being. It would be a mistake to try to ignore such feelings, since such a battle would inevitably be doomed to failure.

It is worth concentrating on the feeling that is dominating us, and attempting to focus on our awareness in order to understand the origin of this feeling and the real reason why it has arisen at this point.

The origin of such feelings often lies in our inner feelings of guilt that haunt us due to our disturbed consciousness. Perhaps we wronged somebody or caused someone harm, and the unpleasant feeling is now taking us over.

Sometimes the inner sensation of disquiet and unpleasantness is caused by a different factor. Perhaps we have been facing pressure at work or in some other area of our life that is making us feel inner disquiet and instability. Perhaps someone has treated us badly, unfairly, or disrespectfully without our being able to understand why. Feelings such as this sometimes cause us a kind of restlessness that demands us to investigate the reason so that we can understand the source of the emotion. This is the only way to cope with such emotions, and to prevent such disturbance in the future.

We should not begin to work on this during the process of meditation itself, but rather try to fathom the source of these emotions. Once we have found the original cause, we should try to remove it from our awareness, calm it down, and attempt to cope with the problem immediately after completing the exercise or at a later juncture. In any case we must not later ignore it and pretend that it did not emerge during the exercise.

## Meditating with colors

During meditation we can imagine various colors and examine what effect each color has on our feelings and our ability to concentrate.

Colors are a very important part of our life. Apart from the quality and cut of the cloth, we usually choose our clothes according to color. Different combinations of color fill our house through the furniture, carpets, curtains, and other items we choose. All these colors reflect our own preferences.

We also tend to describe our mood in colors. If we are feeling nervous, sad, or depressed, we may say that we are feeling "blue." If we feel happy and optimistic, we may describe the world as seeming "rosy."

Colors are certainly a very significant element that accompanies us through life, often without our really being aware of the influence they have on us.

The same is true during meditation. Some people claim that colors can be very useful in enabling us to make progress in meditation, providing a kind of tool or additional means to be used during concentration in order to enable us to gain the most profound insights.

For example, we know that some colors are calming. This is why most hospital rooms and surgical theaters are painted pale green, to instill a sense of peace and calm among staff and patients.

Some strong colors, such as red, orange, deep pink, and purple are considered stimulants, and we often refer to them as "loud" colors.

Most of us have our own favorite color. When practicing meditation, we should pay attention to the influence this color has during our exercises.

In addition to our breathing exercises, we might choose to begin our meditation with a color imaging exercise. With each inhalation or exhalation, we decide which color we want to imagine. This will help us enter a state of concentration while noting our feelings toward the different colors.

We should try to examine which colors help us stay alert and clear-minded, and which tend to bore us or make us sleepy. What colors give us a sense of peace and calm, and which ones make us nervous? Which colors make us feel happy? Which ones excite us and which leave us unmoved?

If we find that colors have a powerful and meaningful influence during meditation, we may then choose to continue to exercise with those colors we have found useful. If one color is particularly calming, this may become "our" color to be imagined while exercising.

We may make this color accompany us throughout our exercise, or only to imagine it at a particular stage.

## Focusing on objects

Meditation by looking internally at objects can be a powerful tool for concentration. When beginning to practice meditation, these exercises are very useful in developing a deep capacity to concentrate. While such exercises are recommended for beginners, they may also be useful even to those at very advanced stages of meditation, who may use them repeatedly to help deepen their powers of concentration.

Firstly we should select a particular object and examine it closely. You can focus on any object in the room, but the best idea is to choose one that you can draw closer to you so that you can examine it properly. Now we begin to learn about all the details associated with the object we have chosen.

Suppose you choose a statuette on your table. Look at it closely. Learn every detail and every line of its contour. Then move on to think about the material from which it is made.

Does it feel pleasant? Is it made of cool-feeling material? Soft or hard? What is its texture — is it smooth or rough? How big is it — can we hold it one hand or do we need to use both hands? How heavy is it — can we lift it easily or does it weigh us down? Lastly, we should also internalize our attitude toward the object: does it make us feel empathy? Do we appreciate its characteristics, its virtues, and beauty?

After closely examining the object and getting to know its every detail, we may then try to recreate it in our minds eye. Focus on it while attempting once again to appreciate its characteristics, but this time also make an attempt to connect to the object, to concentrate on it with special intent until you blend with it, as if our consciousness was inside the material of the statuette itself. Through this experience in meditation, we enhance our emotional abilities and our capacity for concentration and insight.

## Meditating on spiritual qualities

In order to focus on the positive aspects of our lives and enable ourselves to behave better in our everyday life, we may choose to use meditation exercises that concentrate on aspects of our character or on positive spiritual qualities on which we wish to focus.

For example, we can choose properties such as logic, mutual help, mercy, devotion, honesty, morality, love, and so on. As we concentrate on these properties and direct our intention to them, our energies will flow in positive directions. These properties will become immersed in our consciousness, so that our sub-conscious will work in positive directions without our consciously directing it to do so.

You might choose a particular property and then examine all its different aspects in your mind. If you find it difficult to concentrate on something as abstract as a "characteristic," try choosing a well-known person from the past or present, perhaps someone you used to admire or still admire, who embodies this characteristic. You may find it easier now to examine the characteristics you have chosen as embodied in the person on whom you are concentrating.

Say, for example, that you choose to think about Moses in order to concentrate on the characteristic of "wisdom." You may now examine all the different aspects of this characteristic as reflected in the personality of Moses. In what ways did he demonstrate wisdom? When? What means did he use? What made them so special?

Now concentrate on other qualities that you admire in the character you have chosen out of recognition and empathy, but not out of blind admiration that removes your ability to judge. Be sure to rid yourself of any element of worship or unbridled admiration. Insofar as you can, examine the personality you have chosen in a rational and objective manner.

It is important not to identify completely with the personality on whom you have chosen to concentrate, since such a total merger deprives us of our own individual ego, with the risk of mental identification with the character leading to the blurring of distinctions that should remain clear. We must examine the character who is currently in our mind through a profound inner observation, with the intention of concentrating our energies on the positive energies of this character and drawing them into ourselves.

## Meditation directed to the supreme intellect

How many times have you thought about something or tried to solve a problem without success?

Alongside those occasions when you were unsuccessful, there must have been many others when even if you did not manage to solve the problem the first few times, after thinking again and again and arranging the relevant data in your mind in every possible way, you eventually had a flash of inspiration and realized how to solve the problem.

Where does this spark of "genius" come from? When did it appear and what made it emerge suddenly after repeated attempts to find an answer proved unsuccessful?

In occasional cases it is intuition that makes us discover the ability within us to solve a problem. More often, however, the solution does not come suddenly, but rather from the superior intellect — that part of our mind that managed to put all the pieces of information together and to send us the solution at a given moment. But what created that moment was the ability of the lower intellect, on the level we use every day; the way we organized the data in our minds and the ability to be flexible enough in intellectual terms to try ideas again and again, turn them over in our mind, and place them in a different position each time. This is what eventually caused the supreme intellect to intervene, and this is what laid the foundation for our ability eventually to light the spark from the supreme intellect.

This may sound irrational and impractical, yet the fact is that the intellect can be exercised on different levels by concentrating on abstract concepts versus concrete ones.

The ideas that comprise thought are always abstract thoughts that go together to form concrete ideas. Two or more ideas can be concrete and yet combine to form a completely abstract line of thought.

For example, let us concentrate on musical notes. What are notes, and how do they create music? What harmonious sequence of notes will sound pleasant and which will sound jarring and make us feel uncomfortable? Bearing in mind our above discussion on the subject of thought, let us try to listen to the notes. Imagine that we can hear all the various shades, tones, scales, and so on. Now let us try to concentrate on the concept "note" without hearing the notes themselves. The notes gradually fade away and we cease to hear them, and concentrate only on the concept itself.

Now let us try to concentrate on the word "odor." We will try to imagine several familiar odors — lemon, garlic, a particular flower, the smell of grass after rain, and so on. Now we will disconnect our imagination from these odors and concentration on the concept "odor." Both musical notes and odors relate to the senses. Do not try to think of them in verbal terms, but rather in conceptual terms. Attempt to experience and internalize them conceptually. Do not give them names or labels, but try to experience them with your inner self and your awareness.

Try several experiments of this type to enable you to reach the highest possible level of thought, so that you can connect to the place that is the source of the "spark" that enlightens you as you grapple with a problem, suddenly enabling you to find the solution.

## Using a mantra in concentration

A mantra is a phrase we repeat to ourselves in order to achieve concentration while meditating.

The sounds that comprise this phrase are important. If we find certain noises and sounds pleasant, they will help us feel positive, calm, and peaceful.

Usually the mantra phrases serve as "hymns" — tunes formed by the repeated murmuring of the syllables that create a fixed formula. We repeat the syllables of the mantra again and again rhythmically, usually silently to ourselves rather than out loud.

The mantra phrases are taken from the ancient Indian sacred texts, and were specially chosen to serve as mantras due to their melody and pronunciation, which create a unique kind of calm when repeated many times, and because they encourage an atmosphere similar to that of a religious devotional experience.

The word mantra comes from the word "man," which in the ancient Indian language Sanskrit means "to think." Usually each mantra has its own meaning in the Indian language, although this is not always known. The Western ear mainly absorbs the sounds of the mantra, which are no less important than its meaning. We may often find that when we repeat a particular word many times it becomes meaningless to us, and all that remains is a sound.

The same is true of the mantra: its sound is stronger than its meaning. Even if we have no idea what the precise meaning of the word is, if indeed it has any meaning we can always experience its sound.

The mantra is usually given by the teacher. The world of meditation includes different schools, and each teacher has his own method for teaching mantras to students. Some work with only a single mantra, which they inculcate in their students, while others argue that a different mantra will be appropriate for each student, and therefore provide each student with their own personal mantra.

Speaking the mantra awakens our consciousness and helps us to be attentive and focused. The mantra helps us reach a state of deep concentration. Our inner attention to the repetitive rhythm, the fluctuations of the voice, and the sound the mantra creates within us helps us to pass over the thoughts that float through us until they disappear. We are involved in pronouncing the mantra and in the inner listening it inspires in us.

The mantra also has a physical influence on the body, not only on the soul. It helps the body achieve the level of physical peace and calm it requires in order to begin the concentration exercises.

One of the best-known mantras used by many meditators throughout the world, is "Om mani padme hum." One of the possible ways this phrase may be interpreted is *"the blessing of the contemplation that lies in the lotus."*

Most mantras contain the word Om, which is the sum of all the sounds and voices in the world. Some meditators use just the word Om on its own as a mantra, without any additions.

### What does Om represent?

Om is a concept. It is not anything concrete. Rather like the way we approach the concept of the Divinity, it may be defined as a symbol expressing a particular idea of wholeness, the perfection of the universe, the noblest part of each person, each animal, and each inanimate object in the world.

Om is realized in our inner being and life and touches our consciousness.

As mentioned, the word Om is the sum of all the sounds in the universe. It begins with the sound "o," which is the primitive sound, and the most basic sound that can be made by any living thing, stemming from the base of the throat. Then it rolls forward through our mouth until our lips close and close the movement of sound, thus making the "m" sound. The word Om is effectively the unification of all the sounds we produce.

## Meditation through imagination

Sometimes we suffer from physical or psychological disturbances that meditation exercises may help us to overcome. While practicing concentration, we should try to think in detail about the opposite, corrective phenomenon to balance the problem we face.

For example, if we are suffering from constant pains in our legs that are causing us to limp, we should imagine a completely healthy leg, free of any pain. We could imagine ourselves walking quickly and painlessly, and even running.

If the problem is an emotional pain, psychological pressure, or depression, we should imagine ourselves in pleasant and happy situations free of tension and worries. We might recall our childhood days when everything was so much clearer and safer, or any other situation that includes the solid mental basis that has been impaired.

Remember that while concentrating you must imagine the situation you are entering in every detail in order to ensure that the volume of the imagined experience can permeate your entire being.

For example, if we are suffering from repeated rheumatism, we might imagine ourselves going for a walk in an enchanted landscape that particularly appeals to us, such as islands in the middle of the ocean with soft, white beaches, coconut trees, and clear water shifting in shades of blue, green, and turquoise. We walk barefoot along the sand and allow our body — naked or clothed only in a swimsuit or other light garment — to soak up the sun that caresses us with its warm rays. We succumb to the warm sunshine and feel it penetrate our body and our bones, reaching into our joints. In our imagination we have no pain in our joints. On the contrary, we move freely, run along the warm sand and roll in it, feeling its pleasant touch on our bare skin. Now we lie on the sand, our feet caressed by the lapping waves. We feel each of our bones sink into the sand, our joints resting pleasantly and comfortably.

Now we may imagine ourselves rising up with ease from our rest and entering the water. We feel the cool water on our body. Nowhere do we feel pain. We concentrate only on the pure joy of our body touching sand and water, and on the beautiful and powerful hues of the landscape around us. We may continue to imagine in this way until our body tells us to stop. When we emerge from this experience, we will still be accompanied by fragments of visions from our imaginary journey, and needless to say the physical and inner mental sensations that accompanied our trip to the realms of fantasy will remain with us. We can absorb these sensations inside us to be returned to again and again at will.

Having returned to reality, our real pains will also undoubtedly return. However, we may find that this exercise has an impact on us, in the long term even if not immediately. The calming experience we enabled our body to feel will help us free ourselves of the tension that accompanies prolonged pain; this in itself can bring considerable relief while we wait for the process of complete healing to take place through conventional means under the care of a physician.

In coping with mental problems or pressures, similar exercises may also be used. Here, however, we will focus on our state of mind, imagining constructive mental situations that can blend with our existing ego.

## Are there any threats or dangers in meditation?

As we engage in profound matters of the soul and penetrate the depths of our consciousness and understanding, is there not a danger that we may cause mental damage to ourselves? How can we distinguish between meditation and feelings and emotions that may be dangerous to us?

There can be no doubt that whenever we involve ourselves profoundly in matters of the soul we may reach sub-conscious levels and relive repressed memories or experiences that we have hitherto preferred to bury. Naturally we sometimes do this unwittingly in order to avoid the need to cope with unbearable matters or disturbances that would otherwise prevent us from functioning in everyday life.

Phenomena such as these may certainly arise as we address our inner being. This is a vague yet present threat that should not be ignored.

Firstly, however, it is vital that we feel profoundly that we are ready to embark on the journey into the deep examination of the soul that is meditation, just as we need to feel that we are mentally prepared to cope with a thriller or horror movie at the theater. We must be fundamentally aware of our ability to cope with the danger we will confront.

It should be recalled that the "danger" inherent in meditation is similar to the risks we take in other areas of life. We must look at it in the right proportions. As long as we practice meditation according to the stages outlined in this book, at an appropriate pace for ourselves, in full awareness and clear knowledge of what we are doing, there is no danger.

Meditation intensifies our awareness, not the reverse. We must certainly bear in mind that meditation is certainly not a way to escape from reality or rise to other spheres. Despite what many people think, it is not a way to enter a "trance" and it does not take us to hidden worlds that disconnect us from our existential being. The opposite is true. Meditation helps us to remain connected to the here and now, to be alert, and to maintain sharp and fresh senses.

Meditation enables us to improve our ability to concentrate in life in general, thus reducing the number of minor events during the day that we hardly notice, such as when we forget where we put the car keys or whether the meeting we just scheduled with a colleague is for Tuesday or Wednesday. Meditation improves our ability to function in all aspects of everyday life.

## Meditating with open eyes

Most people who practice meditation prefer to do so with their eyes closed, since this makes it easier to concentrate, to look inside ourselves, to focus on a particular object, and to ignore distractions.

Even when our eyes are open, we can still focus on our inner soul, but we must first go through another stage of practice to enable us to do this as easily as when our eyes are closed. Open eyes are inevitably more aware of the environment. It is harder to cut ourselves off from things around us when our eyes are open and to reach the same profound inner experience that we hope to achieve during our exercises. On the other hand, keeping our eyes open helps us remain in touch with the world around us, and eventually to achieve a more alert and conscious state of meditation.

There is no way to "escape" the world around us. Even when we meditate with our eyes closed we are conscious and aware of factors of time and place, and this is obviously all the truer if we leave our eyes open. We are always in a static situation that binds us to the environment, and this prevents the risk of our becoming cut off from existential reality around us.

Meditation means exploring the reality in which we live, not ignoring it or escaping from it. This is why it is sometimes advantageous to meditate with our eyes open. If we encounter distractions during the exercise, such as noises, objects moving around us, or unpleasant physical sensations (itching, "pins and needles" and so on) we may find it harder to overcome these problems when our eyes are open, but we must try to look at these distractions as an outside observer, and to wait for them to pass.

We should not resist these distractions or let them arouse negative reactions within us. We must accept these disturbances with resignation as part of the world in which we live and learn to get on with them, even though this may sometimes seem impossible. These disruptions should be seen as waves that cause fluctuations in calm water, but then gather inside themselves and eventually disappear.

We can view these distractions as an opportunity to test our state of inner calm. If we have achieved the desired state, these distractions will not bother us too much, and will pass of their own accord.

If the distractions bother you so much that you stop the exercise and become tense or frustrated, this shows that you have not achieved the proper level of calmness. This in itself should be seen as a positive experience that will eventually enable us to move another step forward along the path of meditation.

## Persistence: One step at a time

The desire to practice meditation did not suddenly occur to you for no reason. Something inside you told you that you have the potential to live a fuller, richer, and more profound life and to make the most of your hidden talents and abilities. Once you have started to walk down the path toward the "light" and to look in this direction, the only possibility is to continue onward.

We must approach our exercises in a state of awe, feeling uplifted, willing, and full of love. We must move slowly and persistently down the road we make for ourselves. If we sense that we are going the wrong way, we can come back and try again, without diverting ourselves from the main task. We will not go too fast.

The pace at which we make progress is extremely important. Everyone has their own pace, and must listen to their own inner self. If you "run" along, you will fail to make the most of your abilities, and will eventually be unable to achieve harmony, insight, and completeness. On the other hand, if you hold yourself back from moving at the right pace for yourself, you may end up creating superfluous obstacles. You have to move forward step by step at the right pace for you. You have to open up to the inner source of your energies with love, insight, and thought.

Remember the "basic law" of spirituality: in the final analysis, we are looking for the same things — love, freedom, independence from the will of others, and so on. These are basis needs that everyone wishes to achieve.

If you deprive your fellow human of these basic needs, or if you prevent him or her from achieving them through controlling others, limiting their movements or abusing them for your benefit, you are inviting threats and dangers.

Failure to move in the true spiritual path will bring spiritual ruin down upon you. You will never win through such an approach. The foundation for realizing your own spirituality is to find the giving part of yourself, and to act joyfully, honestly, and genuinely to do good.

In order to succeed in life and achieve the goals to

which you aspire, you must be focused. You must be able to make decisions, realize them, and persist in working to achieve them. To do this you must be aware of your needs and abilities, your character, and the extent of your own ambitions. When all these become clear to you, you will be able to concentrate better and achieve your goals more easily.

You must achieve a state where your whole being concentrates on working in a single direction. When the goal is clear and your desires are coordinated rather than divided and confused within you, you will be able to cope more easily with distractions or deviations. Conflicting desires or goals are an obstacle that will lead to inner civil war, preventing any chance of achieving true meditation. Only through harmony within yourself and harmony with the world in which you live can you achieve genuine results.

## What is "enlightenment?"

The truth is that there is no clear definition of "enlightenment," just as there is no defined goal for meditation.

In his book "Asia's Light," Irwin Arnold writes that the nature of consciousness during the process of its comprehension cannot be defined in human words. Enlightenment is not something to be achieved, and the person who reaches this state does not say that he knows this.

When an experienced meditator who practices frequently and achieves a profound level of thought reaches the highest spheres of his range of consciousness and the borders of his intellectual capacity, and then continues to explore further, he enters a mental state on the highest level, or even beyond, on the cognitive scale of his capabilities. This mental situation enables him to experience a kind of disconnection from his existential being, a fleeting experience of forgetting the self within which he exists. In such a state the physical borders that limit us, and the concrete restrictions of our opinions, desires, and experiences, no longer influence us.

This direct and immediate giving up of the self is an example of touching what we defined in an earlier chapter as the "supreme intellect." This inspiration or channeled intuition may be defined as "enlightenment." This is that inner space within us that experiences reality and brings us to the peak of spiritual realization when we become aware of our own existence and of the universe around us.

## Trans-corporeal existence

Who are we really, beneath all the physical and mental layers? If we look closely at each of the parts of our body, even the tiniest part, we slowly come to feel that we are losing the sensation that this is our body. We start to feel that the part we are looking at is something independent of ourselves.

For example, look at one of your fingers for a long time. Examine the wrinkles and color of the skin, the length of your finger, and the nail at the end. After a long period of examination, you will feel that it is quite strange that what you are looking at is part of your body. You are looking at the finger, not at yourself.

We can also look at our inner selves in the same way.

Let us examine our mind the same way we looked at our finger. Our mind includes emotions, cognitive abilities, and so on. Are mental capacities such as logic, daring, anxiety, joy, etc., actually us?

So who are we, then?

Like each organic part of our body, our intellect includes a range of things. The same applies if we look at our body as a whole; it is just our vessel. The actions it performs, the movements it makes, and the thoughts it thinks are done by our body. I can watch my body doing all these things.

I am not that body that walks along performing all the daily actions that I can observe in myself, just as others can observe in me. People cannot speak ill of me, condemn me, or love me, since they are acquainted solely with my outer shell. Who am I after removing this shell?

After removing the layers that surround us, we discover our true character, and then can answer this question for ourselves.

Having removed the external shells, we can now seek to define what remains underneath. We cannot do this with the human means available to us, since this will inevitably imply intellectual thought, thus creating a paradox and a vicious circle: We cannot use intellectual concepts to move beyond the intellect, since in doing so we are inevitably confined by the limits of our intellect.

Our intellect is there for us to use, but it is not us. Why is it so important to probe this question? In order to enable us to overcome our physical limitations, including our intellect.

The soul within us is capable of breaking out of its confines and soaring to distant planes. Our soul is connected to the divine spark within each of us. While our intellect is limited by our capacities of logic and discernment, our soul can reach the areas beyond our existential physical limitations. It is soul that we use to experience truth in an immediate way, without the need for interpretations that move into the conscious plane through the parts of our body, such as the sense or the intellect.

## The freedom to choose

The more we persist in our spirituality and believe in infinite and eternal life, the closer we will be to achieving our objectives and succeeding. The higher you aim and the more you concentrate on matters beyond human life, the more easily you will achieve the things for which you long.

You must fill yourself with a genuine belief in eternal life. Be open to the world and the universe. Create positive tracks for your energies and enable them to flow freely at their own pace. Let your imagination carry you away to distant provinces allowing you conceptual and conscious openness at the highest possible level.

Remember that if you want to, you can meditate not only at a given time of the day as you choose, but also fill your whole life with a way of thinking and looking at the world based on a constant examination of your inner self.

A Buddhist sage by the name of Damhapada described the essence of meditation in his own unique way: "Meditation is the path to eternity; lack of introspection is the path of death; those who engage in introspection never die; those who do not do so are already considered dead."

## What is character?

The prosaic definition is that character is the sum total of all the mental and spiritual qualities of an individual, as reflected in their actions and behavior. It is our character that builds our personality.

When we want to say that a particularly person is weak and soft, lacking firmly-held opinions, or that someone gives in too easily and does not know how to put his or her foot down, we often say that they "have no character." Someone who expresses their own views forcefully and strongly is said to "have a strong character."

Character is the way we reflect our inner selves, the soul inside us, in our everyday life. The way each of us responds to life after absorbing and examining it reflects our character. The manner in which we respond to stimuli, the decisions we make, and the ways we act in response to these stimuli are all products of our character and of the structure of our inner soul.

Someone who has character does not act as a passive agent responding to the surrounding environment, but alters the environment to meet their needs. Ideals and principles are important components in our character that guide us in our daily functioning as we move to achieve various goals. A person who has character and is neither passive nor active, who manages to change events around them and influence their environment is essentially a positive person who contributes to the environment and leaves their own mark.

Some people have a dominant and powerful character. Such people have leadership capabilities or the ability to achieve significant change in their environment, to engage in impressive activities, and to motivate others to act. While such people are few and far between, each society has such people, who stand out immediately. These people include those who have made their mark on history and changed the face of the world. Others have become famous because their strong character made them adhere to a particular ideological path and to a great idea without betraying their ideals. Others managed to maintain their purity through their strength of character, despite powerful temptations. These are just a few examples.

It is the inner self that ultimately dictates what each of us chooses for ourselves.

Persistence and loyalty to our soul and spirit, the components of our inner self, are the factors that determine our abilities, desires, and the forces that guide us as we move through the world.

The inner soul is the source of our positive energies. These energies may be radiated outward and used in working to achieve our goals in life. The spirit and soul are the guardians of love, compassion, understanding, and giving. These are basic elements that exist in each one of us — the essence of true life contained in every human. The condition is that we carry within us an understanding of what separates us from the animals. If we lose sight of this basic internal awareness, we become no more than animals invested with human intelligence. A person can only exert a beneficial influence on their environment, on others, and on the universe if they are constantly guided by the supreme value of being a human, and never forget this fact.

**Character can be exercised and built.**

The main thing that guides us in building and developing our character is the constant search for the inner light that runs through our inner self like a thread, constantly reminding us of who we are, where our greatness lies, and what our purpose is.

Each one of us has a basic inner character that is ours alone and that defines our personality.

This character includes the way we behave, our intelligence and intellectual capacity, emotions, feelings, and mental and spiritual factors. It is far from easy to try to build, strengthen, or model our own character.

This is a constant struggle that demands that we overcome numerous weaknesses, obstacles, and difficulties.

We must listen to our inner voice and obey it. Attention, particularly obedience in following the path our inner voice dictates are truly important factors in achieving our goal.

## Why is it important to develop our character?

Having defined what character is, it is easy to understand what part character plays with regard to our success or lack of success in life. The achievements we have made so far in life are the direct result of our investment. We are the only ones who can take full responsibility for the situation in which we find ourselves. We spend our entire lives aspiring to achieve more. Even if you achieve success in life according to every possible criterion, you will still set other goals to achieve. This is not only human nature, but it also reflects the fact that without the desire to achieve more and more, and without the push to aspire to greater things, we could not live. Our lives would be meaningless. The entire world is motivated by this same causal power. Each one of us is so wrapped up in these basic "rules of the game" that we do not even notice them, and are therefore unaware that we are living to achieve goals.

We must recall that every step we make in life, every effort or lack of effort, every use of our abilities and every way we channel them are all dependent solely on ourselves. We have the power to control them. If you look back at what you have achieved so far in life, you can attribute these achievements to yourself. But this also means that if you are disappointed with where you have gotten to thus far, you must also accept your own responsibility for that fact.

The more efforts you invest in applying your willpower to achieving the goal before you, the better the result will be.

Naturally each of us has different resources available for developing our own character and personality, since each of us has a personality with different components. However, the more we manage to develop these resources, the more we will be able to maximize our inner powers. It would, of course, be wrong to ignore the influence of external forces. Some external forces support us while others divert us from our course; some factors help us, while others only cause problems. Another factor over which we have no control at all is luck.

Despite all the factors around us over which we have no control, there is no doubt that the most dominant part is what lies inside us, and in this sphere we have control and can determine how things develop.

Unlike other objects in nature, that do not have the capacity to be masters of their own fate, humans are endowed with properties that help us control our environment, exploit it to our own benefit, and take what we need for our development. The more we develop our inner mental powers through persistence and the desire to achieve results, the more able we will be to live a fuller life, with broader and deeper self-awareness. In the end this will improve the quality of our life and make its purpose clearer to us.

We live in Western society, where achievements and success are usually measured in terms of money, wealth, and possessions. The more you manage to achieve in the least possible time, the more of a "success" you are. It goes without saying that this is no more than an illusion. Deep inside we seek meaning in life, and this cannot be reflected in money or other material things.

Humanity as a whole, with all its nations and races across all the continents, shares a single purpose that relates not to the material realm but to values. We all aspire to achieve basic spiritual needs such as love, health, freedom, and truth.

The ability to develop a strong character that will enable you to achieve these objectives lies within you. Only you can decide to realize it.

If you manage to strengthen your character as reflected in your daily life, you will also find that you have access to the material means you need to assist you.

Our character begins to be formed the moment we

emerge from our mother's womb into the world at large, and it continues to be formed every day of our life.

Each event we experience leaves its residue within us. Each experience directs us toward particular behaviors. We learn lessons from things that happen to us. Our senses improve and we learn what to draw near to and what to stay away from; what has a positive influence on us and what a negative one. We also learn from others' experiences. All these factors continually build our world, our personality, and our character. This is what shapes our image and influences our character.

Some people are able to learn more from their experiences, while others do not tend to take enough "tips" from the past as they move forward. We all use the knowledge and resources available to us as we choose. No two people are alike in character and personality, and the way we should achieve our goals varies for each of us, even though, as we saw above, the goals themselves are usually similar.

Life carries us along beyond our control. However we can determine the pace at which life carries us and control what happens. The desire to act and the need to change comes from within our inner selves. This demands that we make a considerable effort that will show itself in all areas of our behavior: in family life and at work; in our emotional, cognitive, and intellectual capacities; in our ability to give and to open ourselves up in order to give of ourselves and influence our environment.

If we do not aspire to develop our character to the highest possible level, we cannot recognize the meaning of true happiness and the essence of what it represents. In order to make the most of the purpose of life, we must seek to develop our character as much as possible. If we do this, all the rest will follow: spiritual and material success; the realization of our hidden desires and supreme goals. This is the only way to experience the joy of life, to drink from the fountain of life to the fullest, and to make the most of every minute.

Each person's aspiration to achieve happiness must be motivated by their own willpower. Willpower will lead us to understand the world at the highest level of our insight. This is the way to experience our partnership in creating the beauty of the world and the universe on the highest level to divinity. We must strive to develop our insight to enable us to reach a high spiritual level that goes beyond the physical confines of our existence. If we look back on human history, we can see that empires have come and gone. We know of the material achievements of some of these empires from the testimonies that have been preserved. Much evidence remains of their splendid achievements and the great riches they accumulated. The material wealth of these empires has not been saved. The towers, walls, palaces, and fortresses have crumbled. What remains in this generation is the spiritual wealth accumulated during ancient historical times, not the material wealth.

Take the example of the Second Temple period, which was one of the most glorious chapters in the history of the Land of Israel. None of the treasures of the temple remain, but what we are left with are the writings of the Mishna and Talmud, which greatly enriched the spiritual and religious life of the Jewish people. This spiritual wealth has been preserved over the centuries to this day and forms part of the Jewish world. It exists within us and will continue to do so in the generations to come.

When we perform a given task, what is really important is not performing the task itself, but what this contributes to society or to the individual. The result is what really matters, and the extent to which the result is maintained in the long term is the true test. All the resources inside and around us are there to help our inner self — the entity that is revealed and discovered through the work of developing our character.

As emphasized above, it is character that shapes ourselves and our personality. This is why developing our character is the most important thing to which we should direct ourselves in everything we do in life.

We live our life through intensive days, which include a long series of actions, some routine and repetitive, others due to commitments to external forces, and others due to internal commitments. We must feel the rhythm of life and live it simply, without paying undue attention to existential questions, to achieving knowledge, or to constant reflections. It is only through the correct balance of all these components in our daily life that we can ensure a complete and active life. We must find the ideal way to combine the knowledge we have acquired with our cognitive power and to implement this in our life in such a way as to enable them to serve as aids in getting the most out of life, rather than as substitutes for real life.

Everything in our life should be taken in the right

proportion. We should not go overboard in relating to any one of the planes of life, but rather work according to a natural flow in all spheres.

The lesson of life's experience is not reflected in the amount of knowledge we amass, but in the way we integrate this knowledge in developing our character. We are the product of what we make of ourselves by ourselves. We are the masters of our own fate. It is we who set our own goals and guide ourselves toward these goals. Nobody can think for us, feel for us, or live for us. We are solely responsible for what we make of ourselves. The more aware we are that our fate is in our own hands, the freer we will be to manage and direct our life toward our desired goal of complete being by developing a firm and strong character.

Unlike other animals, we have not been endowed with our own uniquely sharp senses, with instincts that protect us from enemies, or with colors to provide camouflage and beauty. Accordingly, we have no choice but to take our destiny into our own hands. If we do not look out for ourselves, nature will not do it for us, even though it helps other animals. This is why humans have used their intelligence — the gift that distinguishes us from the other animals — to make tools, instruments, clothing, and many other objects that help us to survive in our world. Indeed, not only have humans survived but despite being considered a relatively "weak" animal they have been able to dominate nature and divert it to their own needs.

The individual is helped not only by intelligence, but also by the inner whole of the spirit and soul, which together form character. Nature caused humans to develop their character in order to survive. We had to develop our abilities in order to be our own masters and the masters of our destiny.

Humans develop, feed, and exercise their bodies; they shape them and help keep their shape. They even develop their bodies in order to compete in the Olympics and to achieve. Thus it is that every so often a new record is set. Sometimes it seems as if there are no limits to human capabilities. The same applies to our brains, intellect, and mental ability. The more we "feed" our intellect and train it, using it to shape our personality and character, the more we will discover its tremendous potential power and become aware of its infinite ability.

### A preliminary exercise for developing character:

Sit in a state of concentration for approximately 20 minutes. Imagine the different events that make up your day and your life. Try to think of the material things to which you devote your time. Which of your daily activities are motivated by physical needs? Are your basic needs essentially food and sleep, or do material needs occupy most of your world and are you pre-occupied with the question of how to achieve something, where and how you should buy something, and so on?

Now concentrate on your mental, emotional, or intellectual needs, such as love, longing, goodness, willpower, giving, and so on. What have you done recently in your everyday life that was motivated by these needs?

Now try to look at the physical parts of your body in a profound way. Take time to consider each part of your body until you feel that it is no longer a part of you. Now move on to inner concentration. Concentrate inside your thoughts and move into your soul. Examine your attitude toward your internal self as compared to your attitude toward your physical self. Did you feel a difference? With which feeling did you identify more strongly?

You must internalize the feeling you experience in this inner examination and assess whether you can implement and manifest this feeling in the realm of your everyday life. As you continue with your everyday life, try to use the feeling of your inner sense to help you in a given event. You will soon feel the results.

You can use your mind to simulate various events you encounter in your daily life and your new way of responding to these. You can focus on these exercises for several days until you feel that a change has begun to emerge in the basic way you approach the world. You may then proceed to the next exercises.

## Laying the foundation for the development of character

Thus we have seen that our "ego" or self is composed of our physical form, including the way we think, our desires, fears, wishes, longings, and all the characteristics that shape the way we present ourselves to the world.

What is important to the representative person within us is how others see us. Our external self is also shaped by the experiences we have in life, and by our skills and abilities as compared to those of the people around us.

Our inner self is our true inner source, without

pretenses or consideration of external appearance. This includes our insights, inner love, feelings, ability to think profoundly, and awareness of our own inner life. The reflection of our inner self in our external self creates the character of the individual. The way the real inside expresses itself to the outside is a reflection of character.

Character is essentially the joint product of these two dimensions and is built by them both. In the case of people with a fuller inner entity, the inner self will usually be reflected more prominently than the external self; these people have a highly-developed personality and strong character. By contrast shallower people with a less developed personality, who emphasize their external self more than there inner self will have a weak character.

Before building our character we must lay foundations that are also based on a strong and firm external self capable of meeting our growing inner needs. The basis of human existence is the balance between body and soul and the energies that flow in the soul. Body and soul can function in harmony if they obey the natural laws of the universe.

If we tune out all the other factors that distract our attention, through introspection we can discern our inner entity and our inherent spirituality.

As with the example we gave in previous chapters, our inner self can be likened to a lake. The more we manage to keep the water calm the clearer it will be, enabling us to see the bottom. The more we silence the inner voices that resonate inside us in our everyday life, such as thoughts, feelings, etc., the more able we will be to listen to our inner spirituality.

When we connect to our inner self and silence the other noises so that they no longer distract us, we will be able to focus directly on that inner part of us that makes us operate in an intuitive manner — not through thought and planning, but through another, more genuine and pure inner command.

Once this connection takes place, intuition will be able to take its place on the "center stage" in our brains, and to activate our external self.

Once this process occurs, we can begin to speak of "building character." The reflection of our inner self in our external self will have built another level in our character on the road to the completeness we yearn to achieve.

Developing the ability to reveal the intuition inside us, to bring it on to the conscious level, and to listen to the quiet flow that comes from it, commanding us to act in its own special way, is the basis for building character in a developing person as an additional step in humanity's march toward a better world and a purer universe.

In order to succeed in our attempt to reach the hidden layer of intuition within our human inner self, we may be helped by the following exercise:

Sit comfortably with your eyes closed. Now try very slowly to enter the kingdom of your mind. First listen to the inner noises, including thoughts, feelings, emotions, and so on.

Now try to focus on each one of these areas separately. Firstly begin with your feelings: do you feel comfortable? Are you hot or cold? Can you feel the blood circulating through your body?

Now try to "eliminate" this focus of interest and move on to a deeper level. Look inside your feelings. What is your emotional state right now? Was your day dominated by happiness and optimism, or did you have negative and unpleasant feelings? Now leave your feelings again and try to eliminate your interest in this area.

Next concentrate on the thoughts that pass through your mind. First look at them without intervening, changing, or removing them. As they come and go, watch them from the sidelines.

Now slowly begin to silence these thoughts and to look at the blank blackboard that remains in your mind. After quieting the "waves" in the lake, you can now look more clearly at the bottom.

Keep concentrating in this way until "something" happens. This "something" will flood through you and give you a sense of being uplifted. This is not a feeling that can be described in words. You can only experience it. Do not waste precious energies trying to understand it or to fix on explanatory labels. This is impossible and there is no reason to do it.

This exercise will give you confidence, since you will know that you are capable of being "close to yourself" in the most prosaic sense. This confidence will in itself help you achieve inner calm and faith in your own abilities.

Now try to achieve a basic state of calm in your everyday life. Create a calm atmosphere in your activities throughout the day. The stable basis of calm that flows in you will have a powerful influence on the future development of your character.

## Belief in yourself

In order to be able to cope with the everyday difficulties that constantly arise in our lives, we must persist with the path that is right for us, even if it is not "fashionable" and even if it requires us to be different and to stand out from the crowd. We cannot cope with these difficulties or with events that require tremendous inner strength if we do not develop this capacity in our personality.

Developing our character sets forward the path for this intensive coping. What materials do we need when we set out to "build" our character?

The most important thing is a basic sense of confidence rooted in courage. Only if we develop these properties can we continue to work to build a firm and solid character.

The ability to remain honest and to have an active conscience is dependent on our basis level of confidence and courage. When we know that we have spoken the truth or done the right thing, even if it was difficult and caused us embarrassment, suffering, or shame, and even if this action might damage us in some way, we are calm inside and our conscience is clean and quiet.

When we are tempted to lie or to commit an injustice, even if it is no more than what we call a "white lie," we are left with a bad taste inside. We feel a storm raging inside us because our conscience is disturbed. We twist and turn to prevent the lie from being discovered, and our life becomes a constant attempt to cover our tracks. We are not at peace with ourselves and we feel "unclean" inside.

Why are we tempted to do things like this? The reason

is usually transient pleasure. Yet is that transient pleasure really worth the feeling we have after we have succumbed to the temptation to be dishonest? We are all humans, and it is only human to stray from the path occasionally and make mistakes. The important thing is to learn from our mistakes and improve our ways.

The inherent power of our inner strength to act honestly and truthfully is the most important material we use in building our character. This is the courage that guides us and help us to feel that we are humans in our own right. A balanced and self-respecting person does not bend over with every breeze and is not easily uprooted and thrown around by the wind, but stands firm, sticks by his or her principles, opinions, and conscience.

Who are the great people, the spiritual giants whose lives changed the course of history and who left their mark on posterity? Those who had strong and well-developed characters; those who influenced their environment rather than being influenced by it; those who were determined and convinced of their own way.

Some of these people were obliged to put up with insults because of the path they chose. They were ridiculed and faced severe criticism. Yet these leaders, those who invented the great inventions of history, and those that fought to the bitter end for their principles, shared in common the characteristic of courage as one of the most important elements in their character, if not the most important.

Feelings that are the opposite of courage, such as anxiety, fear, dread, alarm, and concern, may all lead us to accept humiliation, to ignore our inner command and to be diverted from the path of truth and honesty, as our heart truly wishes through our pure and primal instincts.

If we wish to soar to the heights of spirituality and to aim for those levels that touch on divine spirit and light, courage is our key to success.

We are "lucky" in that our lives offer us plenty of events and difficulties that offer a chance to cope time after time. This is a constant and never-ending test that forces us to cope anew and to re-examine our own courage and character.

It is not only problems and deficiencies such as the lack of money or poor health that constitute a testing ground for our courage, but also situations that may seem to be positive — here, too, obstacles lurk around the corner. Being "too rich, too good looking, too physically able, too intellectual" and so on, are all examples of this.

Our character is tested in any situation in which we find ourselves and in every action we perform. Success in achieving our goals and in opening our conscience and inner self to higher spiritual levels depends entirely on ourselves and our self-discipline. Each one of us has the capacity to achieve this, and through practice we may realize this potential.

By way of example we could practice the following exercise: Think about an event that happened to you during the course of the past day or two in which you did not manage to find the courage to do the right thing and were dominated by emotions such as fear or alarm, which prevented you from staying on course.

Now run through the event again in your mind. Try to analyze it. Was it fear of what others might say that prevented you from opting for courage? Was it the fear of not being appreciated or the fear of insults? Was it laziness, lack of faith in your own ability, or a profound lack of confidence?

After running through the event in your mind, examine your behavior at the moment it took place and how you would have behaved had you chosen to stick to the path of courage. Try to think about how the event would have unfolded had you acted with inner honesty and without giving in to your fears. What would you have "gained" from that as compared to what you lost by the way you actually behaved?

Now decide that the next time something similar happens you will act differently, according to the new rules you have laid down for yourself. If you feel that you have failed once again, do not despair. Try again and again until you manage to succeed. See these events as an essential exercise on the path to achieving your goal.

We now move on to a type of exercise intended to help you develop and strengthen your character:

Try to exercise your self-control. In order to do this you must be decisive, accept tasks, and promise yourself that you have the power to perform these tasks. And you must indeed perform them as required.

For example, if you work in a field where your achievements are evaluated in quantitative terms (such as the number of sales you make in a day), try to do a little better than you usually demand of yourself.

Try to change some of the habits that have become ingrained in you. This is an excellent opportunity to uproot bad habits. In the first stage try to refrain from various actions, and later try to act in a manner that is the opposite of your usual habits.

If you smoke, try to reduce significantly the number of cigarettes you smoke each day. If you cannot finish a meal without having something sweet, this is an opportunity to kick the habit. If you usually spend your time after work on the couch in front of the television, eating, speaking on the telephone, and reading the newspaper while the television is on, try to set aside special time for each of these activities. Eat together with your family in the dining room, turn off the television while you read then newspaper, and so on.

At the next stage try to do things that are actually the opposite of your habits. If you are one of those people who wake up in the morning and then turn over for "just another five minutes" that end up leaving you pressed for time, force yourself to get up straight away. You will manage to get a lot more done and find that you are now in control of time (you will also probably not forget or lose things, because you will be doing everything in a more relaxed manner). If you usually throw your clothes around the room, try to be more orderly — fold them up and keep your room tidy. If you are considered a workaholic try to slow down a little and spend more time each day with your family.

The more you manage to change your bad habits and acquire new, positive ones, the more you will gain control of yourself and what happens to you. You will able to lead your life, instead of your life leading you.

Once you achieve greater control over life, you will automatically feel more confident and it will be easier for you to develop the elements of strong, stable character.

## Decisiveness, honesty and sincerity

All the above characteristics are the result of our ability to be true and sincere with ourselves. The foundations of this building must be made of high-quality materials, not cheap imitations or substitutes. To be capable of developing a strong character, you must know what you want and be motivated by the guiding force that leads you precisely, instead of changing your mind every time you get up in the morning.

The ability to be decisive is the product of the capacity to know what is appropriate for you, what you can cope with and what is beyond your powers. Once you are clearly aware of the limits of your own abilities and of the urges that motivate you, you can establish matters in an unequivocal way and be firm and decisive. In this way transient pleasures, longings and whims will no longer have any influence on your position.

If you stick to your inner faith, sincerity, and truth, you will avoid the problems that come from self-deception. Anyone can act dishonestly and deceptively towards themselves or toward the world around them, but any such act will eventually be discovered. Apart from this, one lie usually leads to another one and one act of deception requires further such acts, until the whole building collapses. When everything crashes down on you the immediate danger is that your self-confidence will be damaged.

This is why it is important to begin your exercises on a blank slate. Leave behind your past actions and start here and now to build your new building on a clean work surface.

Each quality you use in building this building must be constructed carefully and meticulously. You must pay precise attention to every step you make and seek to arrange the foundation stones of this building in an orderly, calculated manner, taking into account every detail. If you really want to build a stable building that will remain standing for years, the materials you use must be of the highest quality and must be placed together in a precise manner.

Quiet, restrained, and serious work as you direct yourself to supreme spirituality and to your inner truth will prove its worth in the long term.

When you start exercising in this area, you must be able to judge yourself and your actions in objective terms. If you are too involved in yourself you will be unable to evaluate yourself properly. Try to "step outside yourself" and look at yourself as you would look at another person.

Developing inner sincerity and persisting in this effort will enable us all to live in a better world.

We must develop sincerity not only toward ourselves but also in our everyday relations with those around us. Truth is the foundation of interpersonal relationships. In the absence of truth, suspicion, deception, and mistrust take over. Societies that are not based on foundations of mutual trust, sincerity, honesty, and truth are corrupt societies. The basic lack of trust between human beings prevents such societies from developing themselves. Once people live in a state of profound insecurity as to the intentions of others in whom they have no confidence, they cannot work together. This process leads to social decay.

Only pure trust and basic confidence in each other can

enable a society to develop and achieve progress and a high level of social awareness.

There is no "exercise" for sincerity. The only thing to do is determine an uncompromising route that you will take. In all your actions throughout the day, especially in conversations with others, be aware of your inner truth. Do not be false or gloss over things. Tell the truth and be honest with yourself and with those you come into contact. Self-deception will lead you nowhere.

This is the best kind of exercise: to keep all the above in your mind and to repeat it to yourself. It is better to tell the truth or to remain silent than to lie.

## The principle of giving

In reinforcing the building of your character, the cement that holds the character blocks together is the principle of giving. Only by removing our own desires and needs, and sensing the desires and needs of others can we work together to create a more complete and successful world where all of us will enjoy a more pleasant life in all respects — financial, social, etc.

The principle of giving should be one of the central principles guiding us as we go through life. In order to be capable of giving we must suppress any signs of selfishness in our character: ego trips, narcissism and any excessive manifestation of self-love of any kind.

Excessive love for ourselves can destroy relations with others. It leads people to humiliate and denigrate others, to be arrogant and to show a lack of appreciation for what others have to offer. The more we suppress this instinct of self-love that lies within all of us, the more we will be able to truly love others, to achieve senior positions without trampling on others, controlling them or oppressing them. By controlling our urge we can grant freedom to others. Each person can then express himself, externalize his abilities and strengths, and realize his inherent potential.

Our thoughts should be directed to the good of society and humanity at large; this will lead to actions that benefit our fellow humans.

When you act according to the principle of giving, harmony, happiness, and love will automatically follow. While these are not concrete or material pleasures, there is no comparison between the spiritual feeling that comes with this kind of pleasure and the pleasure that comes from material things.

Peace and fellowship among humans depend on our ability to give of ourselves, to be aware of others' needs and to identify with them.

Only through genuine will and considerable self-control can we change ourselves. Only then can we transform characteristics that come from egotism, such as immorality, evil, irritability, arrogance, etc., into positive characteristics such as pleasantness, friendliness, openness, and so on. Self-control means controlling our actions, thoughts, urges, and whims.

You must remove any negative feelings such as anger, superciliousness, pride, and so on that you encounter in your everyday contacts with others.

As soon as you feel one of these feelings welling up

inside, put yourself in the position of the person to whom you are talking. Try to see the argument or the conversation from their point of view before you burst out. Try to feel empathy and identification with the other person's position. You will suddenly find that you actually are quite understanding of the other person's desires, and this will enable you both to reach an equitable agreement.

We are often angry with public figures who act in a way that is inconsistent with our opinions. Perhaps someone on the city council failed to act the way we expected, or maybe a senator or government minister has annoyed us with his or her opinions or actions. If we put ourselves into this person's shoes for just a moment and try to see the world from their position, we will understand their motives and reasons for their actions. This may enable us to understand their starting point, to accept the considerable responsibility they shoulder, and so on.

We may feel threatened by the actions or opinions of a public figure. The fact that someone makes us feel this way shows that he or she is important to us. We cannot ignore the person because of the feelings that have been aroused in us. The person's ability to make us feel this way inspires respect in us, even if we find this difficult to admit. How much truer this is when the person concerned is not a public figure but a regular person alongside us who has provoked fear, anger, or bitterness in us. The fact is that we did not remain impassive, but saw this person as someone important.

Clearly, if someone can arouse such feelings in us, then we have something to learn from them. Perhaps they will even leave us with a lesson that we will take with us as we move on. It may be that they even deserve our thanks. You can always find a grain of good in anything bad, just as you can always choose to say either that the glass is half empty or half full. This, too, can and should be practiced throughout the course of our daily life. When someone arouses strong feelings in you, try to understand where they are coming from and to get inside them. Suppress your own emotions, desires, and needs and let yourself experience those of the other person. You will surely find your position softened and see things from a different angle.

It is far from simple to perform this exercise. We usually find it very difficult to abandon positions we hold, to listen to others, and to almost "erase" ourselves. If we really try, though, we will sense over time that our approach to the world around us is changing. We will encounter difficulties at first, but slowly we will find it easier to get inside the soul of others.

Practice this again and again. Even if you do not manage the first few times you get into serious arguments or are hurt by someone, keep on trying the next time. You will find that this leads to reconciliation and calm, and to more relaxed and pleasant relations with others.

As well as more harmonious and pleasant relations with others, you will also gain more appreciation from your fellow human beings. You will come to see that someone you have treated kindly, openly and with a desire to understand and give will soon repay your favor and give of themselves in return.

When we manage to do this, we may find that we are overcome by a sense of pride in ourselves. We must avoid this and try to eliminate this feeling. When we help others, we must think that what is important is that the person who needs help is getting it. Do not think about the fact that you are helping someone or doing something for which you will eventually be rewarded. You must concentrate solely on giving.

At the next stage, after practicing your attitude to those around you, think what it is that makes you angry, sad, nervous, furious, bitter, dishonest, or immoral.

After you have found the reasons for such harsh reactions, try to think of ways to avoid them — how to prevent yourself getting into such situations and to completely refrain from them.

## Exercise your body, not just your mind

So far we have dealt with spiritual and mental exercises. But in keeping with the old saying "a healthy mind in a healthy body," we should also make sure to take good care of the "home" in which our soul is "confined."

Inner harmony is only possible if we maintain a balance between our physical ability and our mental ability.

Physical ability gives us a healthy and stable body and is the basis for all the actions that take place inside us. In order to achieve high levels of concentration, supreme spiritual spheres and the ability to disconnect from our physical body and dwell in our inner world, we must ensure that our body is complete, able, flexible, and healthy.

If we are preoccupied with physical problems, discomfort, and pain, we will never be able to achieve peace and calm. Pain will serve as a perpetual reminder of the state of our body, preventing us from avoiding physical sensations.

In order to protect our physical health we should adopt regular habits of exercise. We should exercise at least twice a week and acquire habits of proper posture that will help us sit for long periods of time while meditating.

Apart from exercises, it is also worth acquiring proper eating habits. We should get our body used to eating the amount it needs and refrain from over-eating, which only leads to the accumulation of fat, obesity, and clumsiness. Proper eating habits will promote the quality of life and longevity, since many diseases have their origins in poor eating habits and excessive weight. It is always a good idea to stop eating a little while before you feel satisfied. This advice is based on experience, and also appears in the ancient sources. This is one of the tips we would all to follow.

Remember that protecting your physical health is no less important than protecting the health of your spirit, soul, and inner qualities.

We live in an era of increasing leisure time. Modern society tends to require fewer hours work, so that we find ourselves with more spare time. It is worth planning how to use this time in order to develop our hobbies and engage in activities that are enjoyable and appropriate for us.

One way to use time enjoyably is to engage in sport. This helps us maintain our physical strength and help, but also gives our minds an "airing." The best way to work our bodies and air out our minds without feeling that we have to make too great an effort is to play games.

Exercising and using our muscles can also take place when riding a bike, playing ball games of all kinds, swimming, and so on. Ball games are a pleasant way to relieve tension. Most ball games are based on teams, which means that as well as the physical activity we also engage in healthy social interactions. We get to know people in a different way than in other aspects of our life, and often games lead to laughter and fun. Sometimes, however, the desire to win may overcome our sporting spirit and impair the fun of the game. The idea of the game is to have some fun time and reduce tension — not the opposite.

If we keep the right proportions and see the game as no more than that, not as a competition or a test, we will be able to enjoy the experience as well as the physical exercise.

Other games that do not involve physical exercise, such as card or computer games, may also reduce tension, provide enjoyment, and let our minds rest. We can enjoy games as long as they remain no more than games. If we turn card games into gambling games based on chance, this will lead to tension, expectations, and over-excitement. We will lose the pure enjoyment of a game and it will no longer be just a "game."

# Love, courage and truth are a single entity

As we have seen, our inner self, the source of our character, includes three bases: love, courage (daring), and truth (sincerity and honesty).

The balance between these three elements differs in each one of us; this is what makes each person different from anyone else. In some of us, the most dominant element is the desire for freedom; such people are guided by their strong desire and are courageous. Others are more emotional, tend to take things to heart and to pay attention to small details that others find insignificant. The element of love is dominant in such people. Others still place great store on honesty and sincerity; they seek to encompass all the knowledge of the world, since what is most dominant in their character is the element of truth.

Yet all these qualities that make up the personality and character of the individual also include a measure of the other two; in essence, therefore, they form a single entity.

As we go through life, we meet different people in whom different elements are dominant. Our ability to understand others and accept them is the basis for any relationship with another person.

If we restrict the movements of someone for whom freedom and courage are the most dominant elements, we will be unable to create a pleasant, fair and positive relationship with them. On the other hand, if we show a generous ability to give the other person space when what they are looking for is love and attention, the freedom we give will be interpreted as a lack of attention.

Only through inquisitiveness and hard work, and only by directing all our resources — emotions, thoughts, desires, and aspirations — to the idea of unity can we achieve completeness and secure the unlimited knowledge of complete spirituality.

We are capable of achieving a complete self and ultimate knowledge, but the basis for this must be a recognition of the fact that we can indeed do so. This ability lies in each of us, since we all have the three elements that go together to form our character. We must strive to achieve completeness, and not ignore our inherent capacity to achieve this goal.

In order to be sure that we know which element is dominant inside us, we can try a short exercise at the end of each day. Think about the actions you performed during the day, the conversations you had with people you met, the thoughts and impulses that went through your mind, and the motives for the way you behaved throughout the day.

What code of behavior dictated your actions? Was it the same code as dominates the environment in which you live and work? Were you creative during the day? Did you have strong feelings of hate, jealousy, love, etc.? What emotions did you reject during the day, and which did you most enjoy?

Try to examine the events of the day from a critical perspective. As far as possible, look at what happens to you as you would at things that happen to someone else, so that you can investigate and criticize yourself and your character in as objective manner as possible.

# Awareness of your dominant character trait

You will need to use all your senses and all the means available to you in order to clarify what kind of person you are, what your character traits are, what aspects you should strengthen and concentrate on in order to strengthen and stabilize them.

If you are endowed with a large measure of love for your fellow humans and the world around you, and act according to the commands of love, you should work to strengthen other qualities, such as dynamism, initiative, hard work, courage, etc. Do not let your love control your life on its own, since the results may be disastrous. You must let those around you be free; "suffocating" love is no good to anyone.

If, on the other hand, you most like order, rationality, and logic and are attracted to the exact sciences, try to develop the 'weaker' sides of your personality: love and giving, the ability to look openly at the world around you. This will enable you to improve your relations with those who have a more humanistic tendency.

However, after clarifying your natural tendency and the dominant element in your character that controls the other elements, you should concentrate on developing the strong elements in you so that you can achieve the goals you set yourself in life.

While developing the strong aspects of your personality, you should try to develope, in the same time, the weaker aspects of your personality.

For example, if your character is that you like order

and rationality and are attracted to areas that are based on scientific principles, you might seek to become an engineer. You could then invest all your efforts in directing your mental and physical resources to achieving this goal. While doing so, though, you could also recruit all your capacities to develop the weaker aspects of your personality, such as devotion, love, the ability to give of yourself and to receive from others, the ability to sense the beauty around you, to praise and encourage others, and so on. In the end you will find that developing these characteristics along the way to achieving your goal is not a burden at all, but was a source of mental support during the process and gave you new and unknown energies.

## Determination and ambition

Some people are motivated by an unlimited willpower. Their urges lead them to aspire constantly to achieve ever more distant objectives and to set new goals to conquer. Such people are extremely ambitious and usually show a high level of self-confidence and self-awareness.

The dominant characteristic in people who are motivated by willpower and determination is the desire for complete freedom. They do not like to be subject to anyone else's control or dominion, and long to decide for themselves how to direct and plan their own life as the master of their destiny.

Yet ambition and willpower are characteristics that are inherent in all of us to a lesser or greater extent, even if they may sometimes be so faint that we can hardly notice them.

There is no such thing as a person who does not have any willpower; we just need to learn to control it and use it in a conscious manner. Our willpower can serve as a solid support for our decision to do a particular thing, leaving the way clear for us to reach our objective. It is our willpower that determines the path we will take and makes us strive toward the objective, ignoring external distractions. It is our willpower that focuses our intention on the target, making the path to the target concise and effective.

People whose dominant characteristic is ambition motivated by a strong willpower may find that they have a natural tendency to egotism and to denigrate others. They must be careful not to be drawn to manifestations of selfishness, arrogance, or lack of consideration for others. Such characteristics are liable to lead to more severe manifestations, such as control of others and depriving others of their basic freedom. A person whose dominant trait is ambition must avoid this ever-present danger that threatens the foundations of the building of character; if they succumb, they will never reach the goal they have set for themselves.

## Giving

The basic element in some people's personality is love, giving, and their ability to impart of themselves to others. The dominant characteristics in such people are usually intuition and the ability to sense others' feelings without the need for words. Such people are able to feel empathy and identification, to put themselves in the other person's position and to use their senses, desires, and aspirations to identify with their fellow. These people are usually generous, and will gladly share what they have with others.

People whose dominant characteristic is love will be guided by love to become involved in the world. Love will serve as the catalyst that will lead them to understanding, to seek knowledge, to be active, and to develop their talents.

When someone looks at the world from a position of love, compassion, and understanding, he or she is completely absorbed in these feelings. This will provide a measure of protection against insults, evil, or the injustices of the world we live in.

Yet this type of character, too, is not without its dangers. In the absence of additional developed characteristics to balance love, such as dynamism, ambition, willpower, initiative, and so on, such people may develop an inappropriate attitude to the suffering of others and ignore the existence of those in need in order to refrain from confronting such situations.

When engaged in a journey, such people will tend to make a diversion in order to avoid passing through poor neighborhoods in order to spare themselves the unpleasant sights. On the other hand, if they encounter people in distress they are capable of giving them everything, including the clothes off their own back, in order to feel good and be sure that they have done whatever they could for those in need. This is not the right way to cope with the sufferings of the world.

In order to make a meaningful and genuine contribution, we must develop other aspects of our personality, such as assertiveness, the ability to control and organize situations, and so on. Such characteristics will, for example, enable us to help run fairs, bazaars, or fundraising evenings to help those in need. This will be a more meaningful contribution of much greater value to others.

In order to make the best use of the character trait of love and giving, other principles should be used to bring the individual to the proper balance.

Despite its profound nature and the fact that it is the cornerstone of our inherent spirituality, love means more than just giving. When combined with the inner forces of honesty, sincerity, and truth, love brings the individual to the highest levels and the closest points to divinity and human unity.

## Intuition and the Inner Light

The more we control our feelings, actions, thoughts, and desires, the greater our inner freedom will be. When our insight and understanding are guided directly and unconsciously, they will make us move closer to our intuition. When we achieve the stage of insight without logic, thought, and the other cognitive actions that separate us from our insight, we will be acting intuitively.

Intuition is the closest thing to truth; it never lies. It is located beyond all the inner screens and leads us directly to our inner self. In this way, even if my mind stores extensive knowledge, I will still have an inner light where other qualities can be reflected. The ability to train our mind to prevent the loss of these qualities is the most important thing of all.

We can invest considerable effort in accumulating and

storing knowledge in our brain cells, but this knowledge will be of no use when we come to solve real problems in life unless we train ourselves to use it.

Someone who is close to his intuition and their inner self is able to achieve levels of abstract thought; when this includes activities and a capacity to get things done, such a person can adjust to any situation and adapt himself to any field in which they work or any place he may find himself.

On the other hand, those whose intuition is very well developed but who do not combine this with practical activities are liable to show signs of apathy and disinterest in taking part in real life. Such people look at what goes on around them as if it were not a part of them, like a spectator watching people playing a game.

In order to be involved and take part in life, such people must develop the weaker sides of their character and activate the quieter and hidden aspects that are waiting to be expressed. Only in this way can such people build a more assertive character and personality and take control of themselves and their actions.

## Imagination and creativity

Some people have a very well developed imagination and experience every process in a highly individual manner. These people are usually very creative. Sometimes they experience reality in a way that is completely different from the way things actually happened. They can imagine that the shadow of a mountain is a mountain, and vice versa. What other people see as solid matter may seem to them to be sounds, colors, sights, and so on that create a wonderful world of imagination and beauty of which only they are aware. They immediately find the spiritual facet of objects they encounter, and can see similarities between objects that other people would feel have nothing in common. Their spontaneity and ability to make analogies are very highly developed. The result of this is that a state of harmony exists between their soul and their physical and inner self. They usually feel that they are complete people, and are free from the inferiority complexes, emotional torment, or frustration that often plague others.

This harmony may sometimes prevent such people from obeying the commands and instructions that come from their surroundings alongside their inner commands; this can lead to crisis. The desire to satisfy all parts of one's personality cannot be expressed in reality, and this leads to problems.

The advantage such people have over others is their ability to undergo the gamut of human experience. Their imagination is so active and dominant that they can take their soul and body anywhere they want to go. They can "get inside" other people to know what they are going through, take their body where there soul wants to be, and so on.

Despite all this, people with highly developed and dominant imaginations must integrate in the subconscious the picture of the reality in which they actually live, in order to prevent their losing touch with the real world. They should discover the right balance in life between their ability to float on the wings of imagination and their practical needs in everyday life.

## Inquisitiveness and searching

The order and organization we see in nature makes us wonder what supreme force made all this come about.

While we may not call it "God," most of us believe in the existence of some force that caused all this order, natural laws, and universal organization to come into place. Most people are not concerned by such existential questions on a daily basis, but accept reality as we see it.

Some of us, however, take time out from our lives to ask ourselves what it is that makes us obey so joyfully. Is it the beauty and splendor of the world? Am I obeying the laws of nature, or am I obeying what other people call God?

Each one of surely has our own answer to this question. Were it not for our basic belief in the law and order of the universe, we could not bring ourselves to understand the world, and we would hold back the inner abilities of our mind. A person who is self-aware and has willpower cannot fail to marvel at the might and greatness of nature that cannot be compared to human strength.

People who have an investigative nature and constantly search for answers to existential questions of this kind will gradually be filled by a sense of faith in the forces of nature around them. and will reach the highest levels of understanding of truth.

Such people will usually have a good memory, and ability to be precise and specific about details, a strong sense of logic, and a finely-tuned ability to distinguish nuances. When these qualities are accompanied by creativity, the capacity for inventiveness emerges. The desire to gain knowledge and the natural curiosity of these people will lead them to engage in experiments and to discover new things and create new objects.

The danger of concentrating on invention and innovation is that such people may fail to pay attention to the human culture that surrounds them, or to take in to account the environmental conditions in which they operate. The microcosm in which such people live is based on their inner world, their investigations, and their discoveries. They are enchanted by this world, but it may prevent their listening to other things that are also out there.

For example, a researcher who manages to find a substance that destroys a pest found in nature may fail to take in to consideration that this process could destroy the ecological balance in the environment. A new medicine might cure one symptom but damage other functions. A specific example is that many aerosol sprays damage the ozone layer in the atmosphere that protects humans from the ways of the sun, thus increasing the exposure of humans to diseases such as skin cancer.

The ideal situation is a blend of a philosophical world view that preserves cultural values and admires the inner beauty and spirituality of humans, alongside progress and modernity that produces new ideas and can improve some aspects of the quality of life, albeit on occasions at the expense of our physical and mental health.

## Loyalty through total faith

Some people who believe in God are led by their religious convictions to perform various rituals that accompany the religious act. This strengthens these people and enables them to feel the divine force within them. Religious people show endless devotion in their worship of God. It is their inner faith that guides them — they are not acting under coercion, but on the basis of a total belief in their way and the emotional impulses that guide their faith.

Other people who are not religious direct their devotion to other causes that they see as no less noble. They, too, act with the same devotion as religious believers.

Any creature on earth that has reached higher stages of development and achieved greater things in the subsequent generations of evolutionary development has done so for two main reasons: either because it had a stronger role model that gave it the ability to develop, or because environmental conditions led it to develop to a higher level (such as the problems of survival in nature or the need to use more sophisticated methods to find food).

Human beings develop in each generation not only because of physical conditions, but also because their constant desire to worship the supreme God makes them concentrate their inner selves on the divine forces. This expands their basic perceptions and makes them aspire constantly to achieve ever higher levels of spirituality.

Total faith leads people to be loyal to God and to aim for the highest levels of insight and conceptual openness that will allow them to make progress.

The danger that is inherent in total devotion to spiritual life and belief in God is that this may lead to inertia, cognitive degeneration and an interruption of the ongoing activities of life. In such a situation, instead of putting into action the beauty and good that lies in belief in God, a "boomerang" process occurs whereby excessive faith can lead people to dwell in faith itself. Total devotion to worshipping God may impair normal functioning in everyday life.

Such people may stop relating to those around them, fail to perform their daily tasks, and show a lack of love toward their fellow human beings. This is a contravention of the basic principles of divine worship. The result will be a process that is the opposite of what they expected when they committed themselves to their faith.

In order to be able to make the most of faith and of daily life, a way must be found to combine the two and not to focus exclusively on either side.

When this middle path is found to combine both aspects, there can be no more complete sensation than that which comes from making the most of life and building a complete character that includes the sparks of divine creation molded together into an everlasting candle dedicated to the human soul.

## Beauty and perfection

The dominant trait in some people's character is the longing for beauty. They admire beautiful natural phenomena that bear witness to divine powers and they worship beauty wherever it is found, seeing it as a divine manifestation on earth. They absorb this love in themselves and thus develop their love for God, even if they are unaware of this.

Such people are guided in life by ideals of beauty and perfection. They do not take account of the inherent inner spirituality inside them, and live completely "earthly" lives, without questions, doubts, or inquisitive tendencies. They tend to "devour" life and take all they can from it, enjoying every minute.

Because it is beauty that guides such people, they will usually see manifestations of beauty not only in things that most people would agree are beautiful, but also in things that form only part of the whole or are very small and would usually be seen as insignificant. They may be mesmerized by beautiful eyes and worship their beauty, even if the eyes are part of an unremarkable face. They may also see beauty in objects that others would not even notice.

When people who believe in the ideal of beauty also have the characteristic of total faith in God and worship of God, this produces wonderful rituals and ceremonies. This gives art an additional expression: while some people can see art as the embodiment of beauty, others will see in it no more than the suggestion of beauty as interpreted by the inner associations of the observer.

The fact that people can give themselves up to beauty in its own right leaves them with a pleasant sense of peace and calm, since beauty is always founded on a basic security and a stability that are also reflected in the inner spiritual flow within the individual.

## Building the emotion of love

In our relations with others, we work on three levels:

Those we see as nobler than ourselves, whom we respect and sometimes even admire;

Those we see as our equals, with whom we tend to form contacts and to maintain relations of equal friendship. We develop feelings of affection, identification, and love toward such people;

Those we feel to be our inferiors; our attitude to them is reflected in the kindness that comes from pity or the desire to help them because of our feeling of superiority.

If our basic feelings are antagonistic, this will produce hate in us. We will be anxious and alarmed by those who are superior to us, despise or resent our equals, and feel arrogance and excessive pride toward our inferiors.

While the emotion of love leads us to open up to the world, developing our ability to give and strengthening our mental and spiritual capacities so that we can make mental progress, the emotion of hate strengthens our desire to achieve material things: to seek wealth and physical satisfaction, to achieve control over others, to gain material and financial power in order to consolidate our physical status in the world, and so on.

Hate restricts our spiritual path in life and leads to mental stagnation and decline.

In order to avoid the negative feelings that inspire and inflame hatred in us, we should learn to "transform" such feelings. In order to develop a stable character and prevent stagnation in our mental and spiritual development, we must channel negative feelings to positive directions and turn them into feelings of affection and love. This process is similar to that described in the chapter on the principle of giving. Try to "get inside" the person opposite you toward whom you feel a sense of hatred. Try to understand what is going on inside them and experience what they are going through from a position of empathy. We must free ourselves of feelings of pride and egotism and let our conscience be "flooded" by new emotions.

If we can neutralize our own ego and experience our fellow person, this will enable us to see the world from their viewpoint. We will automatically feel sympathy for the person who inspired the negative emotions in us, and these emotions will be converted into positive and constructive ones. In this way we can begin to lay the foundation stones for the development of a solid, stable, and aware character.

Only through daily practice in our encounters with real situations where we can implement these ideas can we achieve the goal of developing our character in the right direction. Just as we train our muscles so they can bear greater burdens, so we must train our emotions so that when we encounter difficult situations we can cope with them more easily. Only by confronting difficult events and facing emotional stress can we develop our own mental forces.

Those who live in an emotional bubble that isolates them from the world cannot experience or practice any form of emotional transformation, and will certainly be unable to strengthen their emotional systems.

## Strengthening positive characteristics

All of us have negative characteristics alongside our positive qualities.

Sometimes there may be a discrepancy between the way an individual sees a particular characteristic and the way it is perceived by the environment. An individual might see certain characteristics as negative, while the surrounding society views them as positive attributes — and vice versa. One person may see identification with others as a positive quality, but someone else might consider this oversensitivity, an inability to set boundaries, and so on, and therefore view it as a negative characteristic.

On the other hand, there are some basic characteristics that are always considered negative. If someone sees such characteristics as positive, this means that they have not yet developed the awareness and inner spiritual self to the point where they can understand processes. The basic characteristics we must overcome and attempt to eliminate are dishonesty, insincerity, and falsehood; negligence and lack of motivation; egotism and intensive self-love at the expense of love for the environment.

In order to fight these characteristics we need additional means beyond those described in the previous chapters of this book. We must learn to recognize the positive characteristics that are parallel to each of these negative traits and to develop this side, so that the positive will eventually outweigh the negative. We cannot "erase" characteristics that exist in us; they will always be there. But we can limit their presence in favor of developing positive characteristics.

Our ability to give of our positive characteristics to others and to act positively toward them from within our selves will be our true reward for this process.

People sometimes tend to forget the truth that lies at the inner kernel of their personality. Instead of being loyal to their inner truth, people act according to the image of themselves created by society around them. In some ways, this makes such people the victim of the society that "created" them. Thus people are guided and directed by the desire of society and the way it directs them, instead of standing firm by their own opinions and reflecting their inner self. If such people move to another area or another society, their image will change according to the new image created by the society in which they now find themselves.

It is important that our inner kernel should be stable and firm. The opinions of other people, the way they treat us, and their approach to life should not determine our image. We must always aim to reach the true spiritual core of our personality, underneath all the false layers and pretense.

If we reach our true essence and our pure and genuine nature, we will be able to build all the layers of our character in the only true way, taking into account the inner spiritual forces that guide us and shape our personality.

# Accepting suffering and pain with love

The more accurately, gently, and carefully we build our character, and the better we manage to place each character "brick" on the next one, the more we will find that joy, love, and happiness appear of their own accord.

We feel happy in life when we realize the spiritual essence that comes of love, thought, emotion, and practical life as reflected in work. We feel happy when we are satisfied. And what is satisfaction? Essentially it is the feeling that we have realized our mental and physical desires.

People who are deeply involved in their world, devote time and energy to their work, and enjoy the hard effort they invest will be joyful and happy.

As our spiritual development progresses in the right direction and at the right pace, we will feel the results not only in our general spiritual state, with a sense of uplifting and purity of thought and emotion, but we will also feel the difference in our physical state. Pain is a symptom of an existing problem. If we feel pain, suffer, or face distress, this is a sign that something in our present situation is not as it should be.

Pain comes from overemphasizing a particular negative characteristic or from the development of such a characteristic. Pain is a warning sign to prompt us to examine where we have gone wrong in implementing the three guiding elements of human development and of ourselves as individuals: action, love, and the accumulation of knowledge.

Pain and suffering make us return to our inner soul and spirituality in order to put right what needs mending. We might see pain as our personal bodyguard, warning us of the "danger" of deviating from the right path.

Each one of us expresses our faith in a different way. Some people believe in God, and although we may call the force we believe in "Nature" or any other name instead of "God," most of us have an inner belief in some force that guides the universe.

Humanity has established rules that determine the way the universe works. There are universal rules of law and order that humanity follows. These rules are not arbitrary, but are based on an inner intuition as to what is right and what is wrong; what is just and what is unjust. Every person has a natural tendency to absolute justice. As we develop our character, we must learn to stand under the light of absolute justice, and to try to judge things according to absolute justice rather than transient moods.

We usually tend to feel a sense of impotence when faced by pain and suffering, but we must learn to accept these experience joyously, since as we have seen their purpose is merely to warn us that we might be veering from the true path. We must take joy in these feelings and understand that had we not been warned of what was happening, we would be in a truly sorry state. Even when we encounter difficult situations, we must not launch an attack on them, but accept them as part of the divine and spiritual experience in order to correct our path.

If we become irritable, confused, angry, or anxious, our character traits and our inner strength will be weakened.

Avoid placing the blame directly on those around you. Blaming others means criticizing the way they behaved. You must take responsibility for your own actions, since you surely played a part in whatever happened to you. Blaming others is no more than a waste of the energy and forces you need to develop your personality and character.

Do not surrender to pain and do not let it overwhelm you. Learn to accept it with love. Remember that willpower, activity and work, love and joy are the elements you should activate in order to achieve spiritual awareness, the supreme self, and the noblest divine perfection.